From Anxiety to Peace

Modern therapies for anxiety

Timeless paths to peace of mind

By

Dr. Nick Argyle

A title from Grayle Books
Graylebooks.com

ISBN 978-0-473-22146-1

From Anxiety To Peace

Dedicated to Jacqueline, Iona, and Phoebe

Acknowledgements

My family deserves thanks for their patience and support and I am grateful to my late father for his inspiration as a writer.

I have been fortunate in having many teachers in the diverse areas of mental health and I thank them all for their wisdom and understanding. My understanding of Vedic science comes from Maharishi Mahesh Yogi. I have learned from listening to his teaching and through experiencing the techniques of consciousness he has bought out.

Many clients have also taught me through telling their own stories. All references to patients or clients have been disguised to protect privacy.

Contents

∞ Chapter 1 ∞
Introducing the Many Paths to Peace

We live in an age of worry and fear. Anxiety has become so common as to be seen as part of normal life. As individuals we suffer from panic, phobias, and obsessions. As a society we are over-concerned with dangers in the community. Parents, schools and the media expect unrealistic levels of safety and avoidance of risk. On the world stage we have fear of terrorism and economic disaster. No wonder that anxiety disorders are the commonest form of mental imbalance.

In the world of modern therapy, this is a time of increasing knowledge and expectation. There are many approaches and several of these are making rapid progress. At the same time there has been a renaissance of older natural traditions of medicine and healing. It is important to know which therapies work and which will suit you.

It can be hard to understand the many streams of knowledge in modern psychiatry. They need to be integrated so they can be compared. In this book we see how they do relate to each other and we look to the deeper principles from each school of knowledge. This allows us to see which can be most helpful. We can also see what a life free from anxiety looks like.

Anxiety disorders include Specific Phobias such as fear of an animal, heights or flying. In Social Phobia there are wider fears of social situations and in Agoraphobia fear of panic and feeling unsafe. In Generalised Anxiety anything and everything makes you anxious and in Obsessional Compulsive Disorder (OCD) attempts are made to reduce anxiety through repeated actions or thoughts. Post-traumatic stress disorder (PTSD) may also have strong anxiety components. For some people anxiety disorders appear in episodes lasting weeks, months, or years. For others there is a tendency to anxiety which is always present to some degree. Anxiety becomes a

1

disorder if it is causing you more distress than seems natural for the situation or if it is preventing you from doing what you want to do.

Sometimes anxiety is an acute reaction to trauma with high arousal and dissociation or feeling abnormally detached. Longer term PTSD evolves to re-experiencing the trauma in memories and nightmares, avoidance of triggers, and insomnia. Obsessional anxiety on the other hand uses repetitive semi-purposeful actions such as hand-washing or checking to temporarily reduce anxiety. Obsessional thoughts, images or impulses are often on themes of cleanliness, harm, health, religion or sex. Anxiety becomes a disorder when it is distressing or interferes with your life. Anxiety can also cause or be a factor in other illnesses such as depression, addiction, and physical imbalances like Irritable Bowel Syndrome.

Anxiety disorders are extremely treatable. They often remain untreated because people are shy of asking for help or see themselves as having an anxious nature which cannot change. Whether you suffer anxiety for particular periods, anxiety states, or you have a constitution that tends towards anxiety, known as trait anxiety, you definitely can find a better balance and peace of mind. You just need to find the right path. Once you start the journey the way gets easier as you progress. One reason why anxiety disorders respond so well to treatment is that when one aspect of you becomes less anxious such as your behavior, or feelings, or thinking, or physical symptoms, this leads to the other parts improving and a positive feed-back loop.

Left untreated anxiety can affect all parts of our life and personality. We feel anxious. We think anxious, even catastrophic, thoughts. Our body has palpitations, shaking, muscle tension, head-aches, hyperventilation, digestive upsets and more. Our behavior becomes avoidant of feared situations. Our relationships are impacted when we start depending on others for re-assurance, or our fears hamper our family and social life. Education and work can be restricted as we try to avoid stress. We may use harmful strategies like alcohol to cope with anxiety which then bring their own problems.

Better therapies have developed from several paradigms. On the biological side we have powerful drugs and significant progress in reducing side-effects. Both Behavior Therapy and Cognitive Therapy

2

have become very well-established for anxiety and depression. There is more awareness of peoples' ability to learn. Education is available about illnesses and what skills can be learned. We have far greater expectations of being able to change our lifestyles to promote health. People as patients are seen to have more to contribute to their own recovery. Their families are also seen as positive resources in treatment and rehabilitation. Along with better therapy we are trying to intervene earlier at a younger age and prevent illness becoming so serious or so chronic.

Expectation is rising rapidly from individual sufferers, from families and from the general public. Therapies are expected to be more effective and a choice of therapies is desired. Patients want more say in their own treatment, to make decisions and participate fully. To reflect this increasing involvement, patients may choose to re-label themselves as "clients" or "users" of mental health services or even "consumers". In this book I use the word "patients" for familiarity and consistency. Similarly I use the term "doctor" acknowledging this role includes other therapists, especially in the psychological treatments. One of my central themes is how the nature of the patient to doctor relationship can vary.

Causes and therapies

There are many different schools of psychiatry and psychology looking at different causes in the mind, body, behavior, and environment. In contrast to the harder sciences of physics and chemistry, mental health theories are fragmented and sometimes conflicting. In particular, the mind and the body remain split. Modern science has created some powerful specific technologies but in mental health especially we need to look to the integration of underlying laws and intelligence. Traditions of natural medicine have in the past presented a more unified view of life with simpler and broader principles.

Anxiety disorders have a strong genetic component with 30-50% of the cause being genetic on average. Upbringing also has a big influence on your learned behavior, beliefs, and coping style. Adverse childhood experiences of separation, frequent moves, abuse, poverty, or

3

just being in an anxious household, all predispose you to an anxiety disorder. Ten percent of the population will have a significant anxiety disorder at some point. This figure is much higher if minor phobias, anxiety traits, or social anxiety is counted.

Psychoanalysis which is very focused on parent child-relationships itself had some interesting parents. It derived partly from the darker philosophies of the late nineteenth century in Europe, partly from the theatrics of hypnosis, and partly from the emerging science of chemistry. Freudian analysis described the unconscious mind and the dynamic interplay of different parts of the mind. Analysis has positive ideas about our capacity for self knowledge but in practice it was not successful enough as a therapy. This led to a decline in the later twentieth century but it had established important ideas which remain valid. One of its major concerns was the importance and positive value of the relationship between the doctor and patient.

Behavior Therapy, by contrast, is very simple and arose from a few principles observed in learning experiments with rats and pigeons. It uses our natural ability to learn and emphasizes that change is possible, especially for individual behaviors like phobic avoidance. It stresses the use of experience and practice of tasks such as exposure. We have the ability to adapt to new situations. There is an interaction between our intelligence and capacity for learning and the intelligence that is found in the environment in terms of cues, contingencies, and rewards.

Cognitive Therapy also starts with a simple approach to the content and patterns of thought. We can use our intellect to challenge these and choose new thoughts. This depends on our ability to stand back from thoughts on the surface level and reflect on them. This is a process of transcending to a deeper and more reflective level of the mind. Along with Behavior Therapy, Cognitive Therapy has underpinned the advancement of skills' training which has been extended for use in personality disorder.

Biological medicine has given us the development of powerful drugs. Its understanding of the mechanisms of illness and of normal brain functioning continues to lag behind. It is excellent for the fast relief of many symptoms but much less good for cure. There is a tendency for science to wait for genetics to produce all the answers.

4

However these answers may be too complicated to be practically useful. We already know that even the most biologically influenced illnesses have only about half their causation in the genes and that gene expression is modified by experience. The effects of environment and upbringing will remain very important. In many situations biological and psychological treatments work together and support each other. We no longer have to think that the physiology is always driving the psychology. Recent brain scanning technology allows us to see how brain functioning changes with mental activity. The effects of psychological stress on both brain development and personality are also becoming known. Among the anxiety states, OCD shows the clearest localised brain scanning abnormalities.

The relationship between an individual and other people is now seen more positively. Families are taken as potential supports in therapy and family therapy can engage their special resources and dynamics. Group therapy and particularly self-help groups allow people to learn more from each other and mutually empower themselves. Those with severe mental illness receive treatment in the community and closer to their normal social groups rather than in isolated asylums. We recognize that staying involved with your family, friends and work are important for regaining and maintaining mental health. The effect of the community or society can be supportive rather than stigmatizing.

Many people have looked for alternative or complimentary therapy from natural medicine which is now a boom industry. This is largely because modern medicine is fragmented. Natural medicine emphasizes the balance between man and the environment and the natural rhythms of life. The body's own intelligence and healing resources are used. A better life-style reduces stress. If stress does accumulate the mind and the body become unfit and a vicious circle may mean that we become even more vulnerable to stress. It is important to keep ahead, with the mind and body resilient and strong.

Stress has become a plague of the modern era. It can be defined in many ways. Some stress is inevitable in life, such as getting out of bed in the morning. Significant stress can be seen as any experience or situation in which our normal homeostasis is overwhelmed. We have strong balancing and repair mechanisms but when these cannot

5

keep up stress is being accumulated. Two of the most useful repair men are sleep and enjoyment. If your sleep becomes disturbed and you wake up still feeling tired, or if you find you cannot enjoy normal pleasures, these are warning signs that your normal recovery processes are overburdened and you are incurring stress.

The benefits of rest can be enhanced by meditation such as Transcendental Meditation (TM) which gives a deeper rest than sleep. Meditation is a powerful technique for going beyond anxiety. TM is the simplest and best researched meditation especially for anxiety. This comes from the Vedic tradition which also gives us Ayur Vedic medicine. Maharishi Mahesh Yogi has recently helped revive Vedic knowledge emphasizing the central role of consciousness.

Should we choose drugs or psychological therapy? Modern medicine or natural cures? In this book we find knowledge to help us choose. Each type of therapy is assessed as to which anxiety disorders it is effective for and which types of people will find it suits them. Key to this is understanding the principles of each therapy and the doctor-patient relationships.

Deeper principles of modern psychiatry and Vedic science

The different therapies all point towards health along their various paths. They can be used to see the qualities of true mental health and nature of the basic field of mental health in life. Biological and psychological therapies are often used with very limited aims. We have to look beyond these aims to see our full potential and true peace of mind. Modern therapies point to integration and self knowledge as important and to the existence of inner intelligence. We can follow these to understand the nature and qualities of the most peaceful settled state of mind.

Insights from modern physics and from Maharishi's Vedic Science help integrate the main principles of different theories in modern psychiatry. Mental health is found to be based on the deepest and simplest level of your experience, which is just consciousness, or inner wakefulness. This level of intelligence is common to the mind, body, and environment.

Unity and diversity in life

The nature of the universe, including life on earth, is to be diverse. The more expressed and complicated levels are more variegated. The biological sciences are still caught up in this diversity and need to look towards their more successful cousin, physics. The theoretical connections between biology through chemistry to physics are solidly established. However biology has not learnt enough from modern physics about the underlying fields of intelligence in nature. Physics has been extremely successful in finding deeper theories which are simpler and more comprehensive. Beneath the complexity of the surface lie fewer and simpler elements. On this journey modern physics has discovered that the underlying laws of nature are a completely different type to those that are useful on the surface.

The basis of the physical body is our cellular and chemical structure. In turn these are based on the particles and energy fields of modern physics and ultimately on the Unified Field. This Unified Field of intelligence found by physicists has the qualities of consciousness. On the surface we experience consciousness in terms of separate and diverse thoughts and senses. As physicists did so successfully, psychologists need to recognize the underlying field of consciousness, in which all other subjective experiences are simply different fluctuations. It is perhaps ironic that it was physics, that most objective and hard science, that discovered the Unified Field first. Perhaps this was because we had lost faith in our subjective experience as being reliable or valuable. The subjective and objective sides of life are fundamentally connected because they are expressions of one under-lying field of consciousness. Our unique human ability is the capacity to directly experience this field. Our mind can easily be aware of this transcendental field because it is the most settled state of our awareness. It is pure wakefulness with no specific mental activity other than being fully awake.

The diversity of life arising from a single unified field of natural law is illustrated on the following chart. Subjective and objective streams of knowledge emerge as two aspects of one field of intelligence. The individual has aspects of mind and body. The environment also has two

7

sides. The social environment comprises other people who also have their own minds. The physical environment is partly biological, linked to the body via DNA and common biological structures, and partly non-biological.

Unified Field Chart for Diversity of Life

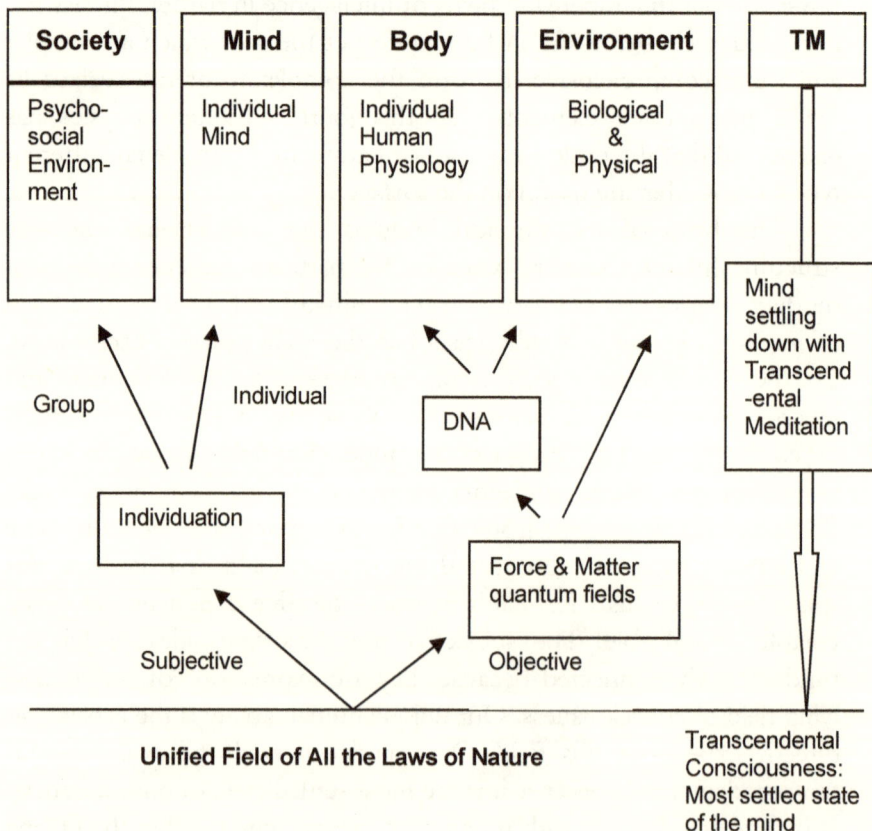

Society	Mind	Body	Environment	TM
Psycho-social Environ-ment	Individual Mind	Individual Human Physiology	Biological & Physical	

Group   Individual

Mind settling down with Transcend-ental Meditation

Individuation

DNA

Force & Matter quantum fields

Subjective   Objective

Unified Field of All the Laws of Nature

Transcendental Consciousness: Most settled state of the mind

The theoretical links between the objective side of the chart and the underlying Unified Field are better understood by modern science than are the links on subjective side. The integration between the columns is also poor. On the far right is an arrow representing our ability to directly experience transcendental consciousness.

We can organise the different types of knowledge useful to modern psychiatry according to the main sections of the chart. These contain the main types of therapy and areas of life that affect anxiety.

The Body

For the physical body scientific knowledge is organised in layers according to size. The whole body is composed of systems such as nervous, digestive, and cardiovascular, which in turn contain individual organs. Organs are made up of tissues and tissues of cells. Cells are structured from sub-cellular components and molecules. Our DNA is not a smaller molecule but it is more fundamental in terms of its intelligence which can be said to structure other molecules and the cell.

We can identify therapies or interventions at the different levels. Sleep and exercise affect the whole physiology. Breathing and relaxation target the respiratory and muscular systems for anxiety components. Our individual organs are less prominent as causes of anxiety, unless the thyroid is over active, but chronic illness of many different individual organs can give rise to general weakness and increase anxiety. The molecular level is associated with drug therapy which is the main biological intervention. DNA is not yet a focus of therapy but there are strong genetic influences in some types of anxiety and genes are being identified.

> **BODY**
>
> Whole physiology
> *Sleep, exercise*
>
> Organs & systems
> *Relaxation, massage, breathing, surgery*
>
> Cells & tissues
> *Pathology testing, Implants*
>
> Molecules
> *Drug therapy*
>
> Human DNA
> *Genetic screening and therapy*

9

Underneath DNA lie the atoms that make it up and underneath them are the fundamental force and matter fields of quantum physics which are themselves expressions of the Unified Field.

The Material Environment

This can also be described in layers but it is more complicated and our understanding less integrated. On the biological side there are many influences from the ecology only some of which are simple like allergies. Our bodies interchange molecules with the environment through eating and breathing. Our diet is the most intimate aspects of our relationship with the environment. The importance of clean air and water are becoming increasingly recognized with the pressure from pollution. Modern science analyses food at the level of chemistry whereas natural schools of medicine often see whole plants as having a level of intelligence which can be useful. Eating food can be seen as taking in solid material but also as

Environment	
Biological	**Physical**
Ecology	Geography
Allergies	Weather
Diet	Housing
Balanced diet	Hospitals
	Architec-
Animals	ture
Phobias, pets	
	Chemicals
Plants	*Pollution*
Natural	
medicine	Elements
	Light, air,
Microbes	*heat, water*
Hygiene	
	Time
Chemicals	*Biorhythms*
Addiction	

taking in packages of intelligence which interact with our own. Diet is a mainstay of Ayur Vedic therapy but hardly mentioned in Western psychiatry.

On the physical side, the weather and geography are commonly felt to affect us. Being in the mountains or a desert or a forest generates different feelings and everybody has a range of temperature or humidity that they prefer. However real these effects, they are difficult to analyse at a chemical level. Even the effects of the many

From Anxiety To Peace

chemicals in the environment, whether natural or industrial, are problematic.

The Mind

The mental world is divided into the individual mind and other people. In this area there is less agreement among scientists as to the overall structure. I have structured it from the more superficial to the deep in terms of our subjective experience, but do acknowledge that there may be more argument here. In the individual mind, behavior and senses are the most superficial. Behavior is directly visible to other people and senses allow us to perceive the outside world. Perhaps surprisingly, Behavior Therapy (BT), which deals with this most superficial level, is one of the most successful brands especially for anxiety states. At its simplest, BT would advise an anxious person to overcome fear through exposure or practice. The senses are not much used in modern psychiatry, except for advice on listening to soothing music, but in popular culture advice on aromatherapy and whale song is freely available. Use of all five senses is at the forefront of Ayur Vedic therapy.

Individual Mind
Behavior *BT*
Mind/Senses *Hypnosis* *NLP*
Intellect *CT*
Feeling *Psychoanalysis*
Ego *Adler, IPT*
Self *Humanist*

Hypnosis is the treatment that teaches various tricks at the level of attention and the senses. It has fallen out of favour partly because of its association with entertainment but still contains some useful knowledge. The analysis of language can be associated with hypnosis as in Neuro-Linguistic Programming. Using different modes of language can help free you up from fixed reactions and patterns of thought. Language can be analysed differently in Psychoanalysis. The intellect is the realm of Cognitive Therapy which is a leading approach to treating panic and OCD, through identifying incorrect and magical thinking patterns.

11

The feeling level is certainly seen by psychoanalysts as deeper and this would probably be common experience, though the intellect can also be cultivated at a deep level. Psychoanalysis deals with the meaning of experiences and memories which requires a combination of heart and intellect.

The ego represents the individual or small self and in Freudian analysis is only one element of the mind rather than being a more fundamental level. Other analytic schools such as Adler's gave the ego a more important role related to power or empowerment of the individual. Interpersonal therapies also relate to this level. The self can be a deeper concept. This term is used in different ways but usually includes spiritual or transcendental aspects of individual life. Spiritual emptiness is a common finding in mental illness, particularly in later life or in borderline personality disorder, and treatments here include meditation and validation of one's own inner world. I use the term self with a small "s" to denote the individual ego which is related to our individual personality and also faces out to our social self as others see us. The Self with a large "S" refers to the unbounded nature of the individual. This Self is experienced internally as the transcendental basis of our mind.

Society – our mental environment

The study of other people is the field of social sciences and they are even less well organised or precise than the psychologies. Even the harder end of social science such as economics is notoriously poor at prediction and full of contradictory theories. I have ordered the psychosocial environment simply in terms of the numbers of people. At the highest level of society the government can take action through legislation and through its influence on education and health services. A topical example has been more effort to reduce the abuse of children which may be a forerunner

Society

Society
Law, politics, economics

Groups
Family, Dance, Encounter

Couples
Marital therapy

Individual
Roles
Social skills
Occ. therapy

to later anxiety or depression. Action against drugs and alcohol has been tried but generally with poor results. Much political thought is given to economic success but the scientific study of happiness shows clearly that it is not very closely connected to economic improvements once the basics of life are provided for. Science has not made a good job of studying society and relationships, and the arts, particularly literature and drama, remain better educators here.

Small groups of people give rise to other natural activities we use to improve our mood and confidence, such as music and dancing and sport. Groups may also be used for specific therapeutic purposes in the various schools of therapy. The family is a very special group and a crucial part of our social environment. Therapeutically we may seek to change the family environment to help an individual or we may use the processes of the family as part of therapy. Marital therapy of course deals with couples and the fact that this has been such a flourishing business pays sad tribute to the stress this relationship is under. Some individual roles relate directly to the social environment and the teaching of social skills or assertiveness can be important in increasing self-esteem and confidence.

What happens beneath the level of individual or group minds is much less clear than the corresponding level in physics. We do not know whether to approach this level from the sciences, the arts, philosophy or religion. Some psychotherapies try to address trans-cendental levels but they have not become a part of the mainstream. Traditional knowledge about these areas has become lost through time and social fragmentation. There has been a lack of sufficient numbers of people directly experiencing levels of consciousness beyond the individual to keep this knowledge lively in society.

Individuation on the chart represents that point or process in which an individual consciousness becomes distinct from the group consciousness. On a small scale and at a more relative level the emotional separation of the infant from its mother has been very much studied and if the separation is not managed well future problems such as anxiety are likely. But to understand this more simply we can take a lesson from the physical sciences. Quantum theory shows us that individual particles and forces are nothing but

13

apparently local manifestations of infinitely expanded underlying field. It seems likely that consciousness, that finest of experiences, would enjoy dynamics at least as subtle. The individual physiology at the material level supports an individual separate experience of life. But just as the physical physiology reflects underlying universal fields, so does the subjective experience of the individual rest on the Unified Field of consciousness which underlies all individuals. This is the Vedic view of consciousness and it synchronises well with theories of physical science. In a more spiritual language we can say that the individual spirit is part of God's wider creation, or part of God, depending on our religion.

The languages of knowledge

Modern biological science predominantly uses chemistry and this language has not been very useful in describing differences between individuals with regard to anxiety traits. Nor does it help much with different sleep patterns, dietary preferences, or how we react to the world around us in terms of changing weather or time of day. Natural systems of medicine have a concept of basic elements giving a language that can describe both an individual's constitution and the environment in a way that is easily understood. Ayur Veda is an ancient system revived in the last 50 years. Maharishi's understanding of the central place of consciousness has restored the mental side to Ayur Veda and a deeper knowledge of this tradition.

Introducing a model patient

To help orient us to the different therapies we shall send out an imaginary volunteer. Let us meet a lady called Caroline who has panic attacks and visits therapists from different schools of psychiatry. How does her consultation vary? The biologist is soon asking her questions, then testing her reflexes, looking in her eyes with his strange torch, and ordering blood tests. Knowledge accumulates in the doctor's mind while she waits patiently for his verdict. She is a rather passive specimen in this scenario.

14

The analyst invites her to start wherever she likes. No intrusive questions, certainly no physical contact or taking off of clothes. The process is much longer and vaguer. She is not passive, far from it. It seems much harder work. But if all goes well she will gain insight into some inner conflict. Panic may never even be mentioned.

The behavioral therapist asks questions to find associations in Caroline's behavior or environment with her panics. Then she has to become more active, doing homework to gather more data. The therapist may act as a model, demonstrating relaxation or how to handle situations where her panics occur.

The cognitive expert is similar to the behaviorist but a bit more subtle. The therapist wants to discover her thinking processes and need Caroline's help to do this. Again there is a mixture of collaborative explanation and teaching, followed by practice.

We shall follow Caroline in more detail in each chapter.

Doctor — Patient Relationships

The doctor-patient relationship is seen as a critical healing factor in psychological therapy. How this relationship is used varies across therapies and can be seen as defining different therapies. Superficially, there are some common useful qualities in any good therapeutic relationship. Strong trust and respect for example allow more communication. But how communication works, how knowledge is gained, and what sort of knowledge is achieved, these vary greatly. We shall analyse therapies according to whether the doctor or patient takes the role of Knower or Known. They can also take responsibility for the process of gaining knowledge.

In the biological model, the doctor observes the patient as an object. The process involves questions, physical examination, and if you are unlucky, blood tests, x-rays and other diagnostic procedures. The doctor dominates the interaction, directing the questions so he can gather the information he wants. Studies show that in general

15

medicine, a patient has only a few seconds to state his problem before the doctor takes over the conversation. This can be unsatisfactory for a number of reasons. As a patient you feel ignorant. It is hard to understand what the doctor has found out. Complex biological knowledge is not easily transferred to you. You feel intellectually dependent on the doctor's knowledge, and so may become emotionally dependent.

In Psychoanalysis, the doctor, or analyst, behaves quite differently. In order to allow the patient to know himself, the analyst does not initiate or dominate the conversation, he does not ask questions. Nor will he give direct answers. This can be very disconcerting, even annoying, if you are expecting the analyst to be an expert, who gives you knowledge in a more direct way.

The biological doctor plays the part of the Knower, his patient being the Known, and the process of Knowing being all the questions and tests. What becomes known here is the patient's physiology and associated symptoms.

The psychoanalyst deliberately avoids the role of Knower. He wants the patient to become the Knower, who knows himself. The analyst takes instead the position of the process of Knowing. He is the lens or mirror through which the patient comes to know him-self. What becomes known is not the patient's physiology, but his unconscious mind.

Other schools of therapy have different patterns of relationships. In Behavior Therapy, the doctor models good adaptive behavior. He acts as an object for the patient to observe and learn from. The patient here is an observer or Knower with the doctor as the known object. In Cognitive Therapy, the doctor starts off as the Knower, but engages the patient in the process of observation, directing him to observe his own thinking patterns. The patient's thoughts and styles of thinking are the Known, the patient himself providing the process of Knowing. In this type of therapy, the Known is not the unconscious mind but the pre-conscious, areas of mental life that can be fairly easily called into consciousness.

Psychological therapies generally try to get away from the doctor as Knower, patient as Known, positions. This has also become a

16

trend in biological therapy. As patients we are no longer so willing to be just passive objects. There is now more expectation of knowledge being given to patients and owned by them. The doctor must be more of a teacher or educator. Written information, and Internet sites have become major parts of medical care. These allow us as patients to have more knowledge and take more responsibility for our own health and treatment. When a doctor teaches a patient, this is a Knower to Knower interaction, the patient becoming an active learner.

In a self-help group there is no doctor. Everyone plays a part in a dynamic where all may gain knowledge. This is predominantly an interaction between two process of Knowing roles, each person facilitating the others' learning. In a group there are many other possible interactions. One person may at times be in the questioning, Knower, position, discovering the details about another, who is the Known. Someone may act as a model or example to be followed, again the Known position. Another person may be good at facilitating the process of learning. Groups also have special possibilities, which relate to the existence of group consciousness, which will be discussed later in the book.

In family therapy, relationships between people are an obvious and central concern. The therapist enters the family group and can take up various positions which determine the style of therapy. He may be an observer of the family, or he may become more involved in the family's communication processes, or he can act as a model for the family to observe. Different schools use different techniques. Because it is hard to be an observer without being involved in this situation, therapists often work in pairs, with one being less involved, even to the extent of observing through TV or a one-way mirror. In general, family therapies recognize the complexity of family relationships and structures. Analysing individual relationships is often not enough. Special techniques and concepts are needed. Instead of directly asking the teenager why she has tantrums, a therapist could ask her father "What does your wife think the reason is for your daughter's behavior?" His answer will illuminate several relationships and possible causes.

17

Doctor Patient Relationships

KNOWER

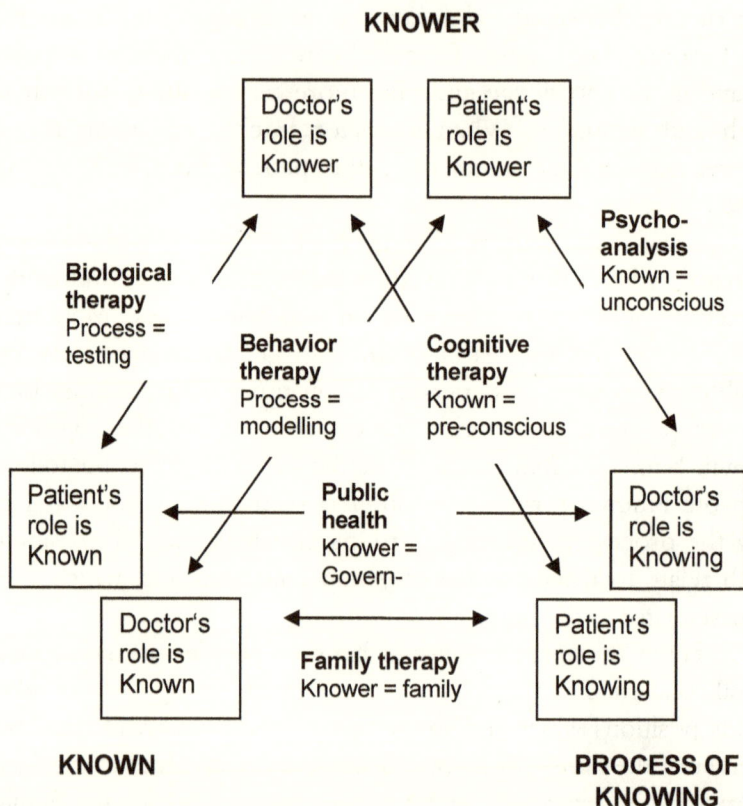

The chart summarises the roles played by doctor and patient in the main therapies. It is also possible for both to have the same role. When the doctor is teaching or giving information both the doctor and patient can be in the Knower role. In self-help groups the dominant role can be the Process of Knowing role as all members help the others learn. In some unusual groups called Encounter groups both may be in the Known role as direct contact without analysis is desired.

Your experience as a patient is quite different in the many types of therapy. Much of this variation comes from the choice of doctor-patient relationship. Are you the passive object examined by the

18

doctor? Or are you expected to lead the conversation? Are you involved in the process of learning? Do you walk out with new self-knowledge? These differing relationships play a large role in determining what type of knowledge you gain from the various therapies. They will suit people with different personalities.

In anxiety your Knower aspect tends to be weak, variable or distant and helpless. Your process of Knowing may be distorted and inaccurate leading you to expend mental energy without benefit. The Known, your thoughts, feelings and sensations, are anxious and fearful. Because the Knower is weak it is tempting to let an expert fill this role to try to cure you. However to really recover from anxiety you will need to strengthen your Knower to gain ownership of knowledge and stability in your Self. Knowing and thinking need to become less rushed, less chaotic, more intelligent. Then you become active in controlling the content of your experience, the Known.

Anxiety Disorders are common but they are also very treatable. We have introduced the range of therapies and the types of doctor-patient relationships. Now we shall examine the main approaches to see how they work, how well they work and for whom do they work.

Introducing the Many Paths to Peace

∞ Chapter 2 ∞

Behavior Therapy –
Knowledge through Experience

Anxiety is most manifest in our behavior. We avoid feared situations or tense up and perform poorly. We blank out when we are supposed to be speaking. We shake or hyper-ventilate. These actions may then make things worse. We start to feel anxious about other people seeing our anxious behavior. If we avoid situations we may feel better at the time but avoidance reduces our confidence and makes the next time even harder.

Behavior Therapy (BT) is the simplest form of psychological therapy. It is also one of the most effective. As the name implies, this therapy is targeted on changing unwanted or problematic behaviors. BT is based directly on simple learning principles and has the strongest scientific experimental foundation of any therapy. This school of therapy sees behavior as being learned and maintained in accordance with a few clear laws. These same principles can be used to change it, and replace with new behaviors. Panicking and running away in response to the presence of a spider can be replaced by remaining and relaxing.

The basics of learning

There are two main types of learning, conditional and unconditional. Pavlov's famous dog salivated at the sound of the bell because the bell was associated in time with food appearing. This is unconditional learning. The association, usually in time, is with an automatic or unconditional response like salivation in the presence of food. Conditioned responses involve learning from the effects of behavior. The Skinner box consists of a simple situation in which a rat learns to press the bar to get food. This is conditioned learning as the rat learns from feedback, from the environment, literal feedback in this case. From these observations and other simple experiments in the early and mid-

21

twentieth century, BT grew. Its principles remain unchanged and have been very successfully applied, especially in the anxiety states.

To teach the rat new behavior a process called conditioning or shaping is used. The rat is rewarded initially for just going near the bar. Then it is rewarded for touching the bar, then for pressing it. Its behavior is gradually shaped to be desired activity. This is a process we naturally use when bringing up and teaching our children. We want our child to be a great artist. First we praise them for just throwing paint at the piece of paper and only later for more accurate or beautiful pictures. So BT is an approach very familiar to us. The strength of a good behavior therapist is keeping focused on the specific behaviors and principles of learning.

The use of food is an example of positive reward to encourage or reinforce behavior. Punishment, or negative reinforcement, can also be used. However it turns out that positive reinforcement is a more effective strategy, especially when learning new behavior is called for, rather than just stopping a previous activity.

The rat can learn more complicated tasks: to run clockwise round of the box before pressing the lever, or to press two levers in sequence, or to wait five seconds after a light has flashed. This learning and progress of behavior is surprisingly easy, surprisingly fast. It is clear there is an underlying intelligence, even in the rat, which displays spontaneous creativity and growth. This intelligence interacts in a dynamic way with the environment. The information contained in the environment determines the associations and conditioned reinforcement from which the animal learns.

BT is the most well-structured therapy it terms of its theory. It also has the strongest connections to other sciences. The pathways in the nervous system that are involved in reward, punishment, and learning are mapped out. The neuro-transmitters involved are also known at least in general terms. The principles of BT can also be linked to Cognitive Therapy and these two therapies are often used together for this reason.

Associations and contingencies can be very complex. Much of the richness of human life, including anxieties, comes from our ability to remember and use multiple and complex cues. Which café do I

22

choose? There are positive cues for favourite foods, views, cleanliness, previous good meals enjoyed. Then there are negative warnings of frightening staff, difficult exits, and previous embarrassing events. I search until enough cues appear to evoke the desired behaviour, going in for lunch.

The scope of BT

Behavior therapy can be used to change almost any specific behavior. In practice it is particularly used in anxiety states. Other uses are for behavioral problems in children, addiction, and in personality disorder. It is most effective where there is a well-defined behaviour or response to be changed. Ideally this is isolated and not enmeshed in other types of problem. Specific Phobias are perfectly suited to BT. These are common fears such as of spiders or dogs occurring in people who may otherwise be quite mentally stable. BT works extremely well here and complete cure would be expected. In a generalised anxiety state where there are multiple and changing worries and fears plus a background level of unfocused anxiety, success is less certain.

A primary strategy is to reward a healthy or desired behavior. Praise and reward a child for doing well - for speaking in public despite being anxious. This can be extended to create longer-term goals and give extra feedback by using star charts for example. One reason punishment is less effective is that it evokes anxiety, anger, or other negative emotions which are likely to make it more difficult for a person to control themselves. If a husband if angry with his wife for being anxious this will make her even more fearful. If negative reinforcement is needed, simply withdrawing positive attention is a very powerful strategy. Presuming that a parent usually does give positive attention to their child, withdrawing this is often punishment enough and even this should be used carefully. This also demonstrates the positive power of attention and the focus of a parent's consciousness.

When you decide different behavior is necessary, BT advises practice and reward. In a phobia the previous unwanted behavior is panic and running away, or avoidance in the first place. This is to be replaced with staying in the phobic situation. Many people avoid their phobias and never overcome them. Avoiding dogs may be okay if this does not restrict the life you want to lead. But if it prevents you from visiting your boy-friend who has a dog, or it prevents you taking your children to the park, you should be motivated to change.

Practising being in phobic situations is called "exposure" and this is the key behavior to overcoming phobias. However you persuade yourself to do it, or your therapist persuades you, exposure will work if you simply do it. The previous response of dog leading to run away is replaced by dog leading to stay. Anxiety decreases and confidence builds with practice. Exposure can be gradual or shaped. Entertaining the idea of a dog could be followed by seeing a dog then coming close, then closer, building up to handling the dog. More dramatic, though less used, is flooding, when prolonged and intense exposure works to change behavior fast - not for the faint-hearted. One characteristic of anxiety is that it builds to a peak rapidly in the feared situation, but it then reduces over time. This means that if you can stick it out, perhaps for up to an hour or two, you will experience far lower levels of anxiety in the situation and learn from this.

So long as you avoid the phobic situation, you reinforce your learning that avoidance leads to less anxiety. After all, avoidance can be an appropriate behavior e.g. of truly dangerous animals. Phobias are by definition unreasonable, unrealistic fears, when avoidance is not necessary. This inappropriate behavior can be extended to ridiculous or magical proportions. A client of mine chose her house and often altered her travel plans to avoid alligators. She lived in rural England and knew intellectually that alligators were not roaming the fields and woods. However her bizarre behavior had been apparently successful in that she never met or was attacked by an alligator. Common superstitions may be seen similarly as illogical behavior magically warding off imaginary disasters.

Magical associations can also be used like a talisman to increase confidence. A lady recovering from severe panic and Agoraphobia, who was now off all medication, found it reassuring to keep in her handbag one pill of each type she had ever been prescribed over the years. She knew they were well out of date and even when prescribed

24

had not worked immediately. But their powerful associations were lively in her mind and this pill collection itself became associated with her continued freedom from panic. While this may not sound harmful, magical thinking can undermine recovery of your confidence if success is attributed too much to such magic rather than crediting your own strength.

Practising new behaviors is very much a part of a skills' training approach. Relaxation is the obvious skill to learn to combat anxiety. This can be muscular relaxation, breathing exercises or meditation. Other useful techniques are assertiveness, problem solving and distress tolerance, which can be learned quite easily. Many people have not picked up enough of these skills through their upbringing. They will like learning and generally find it easy. The skills are not hard, they were just not learned or not used enough. The behavioral approach of practice will often be supplemented by didactic teaching and cognitive approaches. These are aspects of BT that many people feel attracted to.

BT looks at the surface level of the mind. Behavior is identified as the problem and new behaviors, or extinction of unwanted actions, as the solution. The process of learning and change does imply underlying intelligence. In practice, cognition or thought is used to a degree, if only to explain the process of therapy. The power of attention is also used. An important step towards change is focusing of attention on the problem, recognizing the problem and deciding to change. Attention and intention are crucial. The first phase of treatment simply involves recording how often the problem behavior occurs. This attention to the problem in itself has a considerable effect. Just scoring and recording how panicky you feel each day will have a positive effect. Directing your consciousness to an area has a beneficial influence.

To have some fun, apply BT to yourself, and treat yourself like a rat. The principles are easy as we have seen. Pick a behavior you wish to stop, or a new one you wish to learn. Set goals and shape yourself up. Reward yourself. You may already do this quite automatically. After an hour of exam study, you have obviously earned a chocolate biscuit. The extraordinary thing is that this works, even though you

25

are very conscious of what you are doing. These rules of learning and conditioning are strong. We can play with them, play with our own ability to learn, play with our own intelligence. If you are even a bit geekish you can find interactive programmes on the Internet to deliver BT to your screen. Delaying the cartoon man from washing his hands can help overcome your own obsession in this area.

We can also be more aware of cues and reinforcers in our lives which may be shaping our behavior in ways we might not want. There are few things more simply rewarding than free food. This satisfies a basic drive apparently without a negative financial cost. If I, as a doctor, attend a free lunch sponsored by a drug company then I am accepting an association between the promoted drug and free food. However aware of this I may be intellectually, some bias may be set up. This should not be how doctors learn to differentiate between drugs.

Learning is easy

What are the positive principles we see in BT? Firstly, learning is easily accomplished. Changing behavior and learning new behavior is really quite simple. Discovering the available cues or knowledge in the environment is also relatively easy. The potential of animals to learn is much greater than previously thought. There is great intelligence in animals underlying their ability to change behavior and invent new behavior. This intelligence is just not used to its full potential if not elicited by the environment.

The same is true for us humans. We do have tremendous potential to learn so much knowledge and skill but without education, without this being elicited and rewarded, we do not realise this potential. Even basic skills like reading and writing are often not learned, because the motivation is not there, or the opportunity is not provided. Our potential is so much greater than we think. BT is the path of learning through experience. Through experience and gaining new skills greater potential is realised.

Reward is better than punishment

Secondly, positive feedback or reward is more useful than negative reinforcement. While there is a small place for punishment, positive reward is a great motivator, especially for new and higher activity. Animals are active to seek rewards, to gain more and more. As people we experience this as the pursuit of increasing satisfaction and happiness.

One special type of reward is the positive attention of others, particularly that of a parent for a child. This aspect of attention is not fully explained by behavioral theories but is a strong and positive factor. Within an individual, the power of attention is also seen in the beneficial effect of just putting attention on an area we wish to improve.

Moving ahead from the present; not getting stuck in the past

Thirdly, BT is not much concerned with the original cause of problems. Causes may be lost in the past or unknowable. More important is what continues to maintain problem behavior in the present. For Specific Phobias there is often no history of obvious cause. People with spider phobias have not usually been attacked by poisonous spiders. But the mechanism of maintenance is obvious; avoidance keeps teaching the fearful sufferer that staying away from the dreaded object means less anxiety.

Thus, BT is a very forward-looking therapy. Little interest is shown with the past and future change is keenly anticipated. It is also a therapy that gets on with it. Action is taken rather than a lot of talking. As Susan Jeffers writes: "Feel the fear and do it anyway". Just doing things increases confidence. Overcoming hopelessness is important. However bad anxiety is, it is a better choice than remaining hopeless.

Intellectual mistakes

There is also recognition that behavior may be maintained by magical or ridiculous logic. A lady with Agoraphobia was well able to

27

walk down the street, and also able to wear a certain dress. However she could not bring himself to wear that dress in that street because this combination was associated with a previous attack of panic. The mechanism of avoidance reinforcing future avoidance is quite illogical and unrealistic when the situation is not actually threatening or dangerous. In finding the ridiculous nature of these mechanisms, BT sees not only that knowing the cause is unnecessary but also that the maintaining mechanism may be absurd. As such it is not to be understood but dismissed and replaced with healthier behavior. This attitude robs anxiety of its illusionary magical power.

In problems easily amenable to BT, there is a mistake of the intellect at a superficial level. Once the problem is solved it seems as if it was a mirage without substance. The problem was based on lack of perspective and lack of knowledge. A harmless spider was seen as terrifying. Clearly the basic problem is on the level of knowledge. In BT new knowledge is gained primarily through experience. Progress is made through knowledge and experience. Once a phobia is established, being told spiders are harmless is not enough. You must also experience being with the spider and surviving without panic. This is knowledge of positive health. There is much less interest in BT in the negative details of past traumas and problems.

Repetitive and magical rituals are major problems in OCD. BT is a central part of therapy for the compulsive behaviors though success rates are lower than for Specific Phobias. OCD sufferers use repetition and ritual to reduce anxiety short term and this habit can become very engrained, making change harder work.

Anxiety gives rise to excess and unnecessary anxious thoughts and to extra activity. This may be surveillance, precautions, avoidance strategies, magical rituals, or obsessional routines. In extreme cases much of the waking day may be consumed by these. When anxiety is replaced by calmness and confidence, there is less unhelpful frenetic thought and action and so much more can be achieved in the day, with less effort. A more relaxed mental style is more effective. It is also a happier state of mind.

Caroline and the Behaviorist

How does Caroline get on with the behavior therapist? The approach of this therapist is quite straight forward and business-like. The therapist agrees with Caroline what the target problem is. Her agoraphobic avoidance behavior is the main behavior to be changed. Hopefully the panic attacks will lessen naturally as her confidence returns. If not they may become a secondary target. The therapist asks questions directed at the details of how much and how often she can still go out, what she avoids, and the associations and triggers. What helps her to go out? She mainly avoids crowded public places from which she cannot leave quickly, the worst being those railed-in check-out lines at super-markets. Her cell phone has been a great help as a method of potentially calling for help.

The next step is asking her to collect more information by keeping a diary of when she goes out, when she avoids and any triggers, associations and consequences. There is education about the nature of phobias and their maintenance. The core of the therapy consists of an agreed plan to gradually increase how much she goes out. This may be aided initially by the company of others, including the therapist, and by relaxation methods. Friends or relatives can become useful proxy therapists.

Patient as Knower - Doctor as Known

A characteristic feature of BT occurs when the therapist goes out with Caroline. Here the therapist models correct behavior in this case just going out in public crowded places. For a spider phobia the therapist would model handling a spider. The therapist offers himself as an object for Caroline to observe and then copy. He is clearly in the position of the Known with Caroline the Knower.

Behavior Therapy

Knower, Knowing and Known in Behavior Therapy

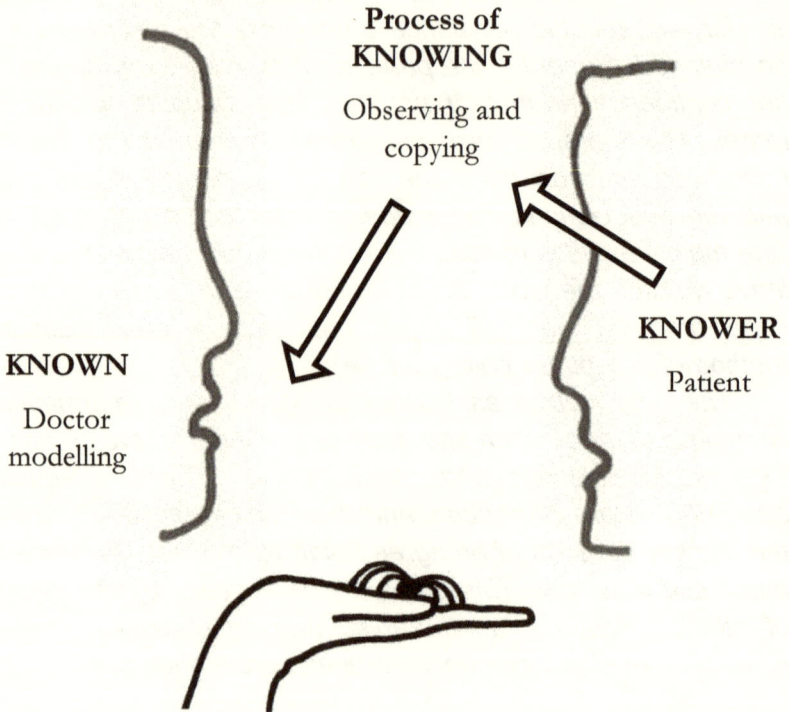

**Process of
KNOWING**

Observing and
copying

KNOWN

Doctor
modelling

KNOWER

Patient

This reversal of the classical doctor to patient relationship, when the doctor observes the patient and retains the knowledge, is very powerful. I once made a home visit to a man in his sixties with severe Agoraphobia. He had become house-bound several years ago and his family were now concerned he had become depressed. Whatever the original cause - perhaps his mother's death - there did not now seem to be any current stresses other than those generated by the Agoraphobia itself. I insisted he would be able at least to walk once round the block with me. Much to his own and the family's surprise, he did so. Thereafter he made quite a speedy recovery with his family

30

supporting a program of outings and with very little interference from myself. Giving him someone to behave normally alongside and to be observed by him led to the experience of going out himself and this was a sufficiently powerful combination to trigger his recovery.

There is a further Knower role for Caroline. The therapist knows the logic and process underlying BT and passes this along to Caroline as education. Caroline was then asked to observe and record her own behavior. She is the observer, Knower, of her behavior and is given a method by which to do this.

So BT is good at putting the patient in the Knower position through education and through encouraging the observation of desired behavior, with modelling by the therapist. After a successful course of BT the patient walks away not only with her target behavior changed but also with the knowledge of how to apply BT to herself in the future. She is able to encompass all three roles, Knower, Knowing and Known and be her own therapist. At this stage the knowledge of how to apply BT has itself become known to the patient. At a surface level she is the observer of her own behavior. Now from a deeper level she can observe this whole process of observation and change.

BT can be called mindless and brainless. In its purest form there is minimal interest in the subjective experience of the patient. Behavior is the focus with better more rewarding activity leading to better experience. Nor is there interest in the working of the patient's brain. The patient, or indeed rat, is a black box whose inner workings are unknown. BT merely considers the inputs - those situations, cues, rewards etc. - and outputs - behaviors. The inner workings of the brain or mind do not need to be known, only the simple laws connecting inputs and outputs, situations and behaviors.

BT therefore particularly suits people who are less strong in the Knowing aspect which includes intellectual and verbal skills. Too much thinking and talking can actually impede the process. However, it may also be suitable to someone who is weak in the Knower aspect. If you tend to look to others to solve problems for you it can be very nourishing for you to learn and develop confidence from your own experience.

31

As behavioral principles work well with animals, clearly higher mental function is not required. Subjective experience, understanding, and even cooperation are not essential. BT can be applied even to people against their will and may be applied without their full knowledge, for example with young children or older people with dementia. As Caroline experienced, the therapist of course prefers to explain, educate, and gain her co-operation. Considering the complexity of subjective experience can enhance this therapy but is not central to it. This shows another interesting point about our intelligence, that we can use it without being intellectually aware that we are doing so.

Human learning

Man is distinct from animals because he has increased conscious experience and mental abilities. We can learn through more abstract processes. Sometimes these higher functions are less unavailable. This occurs in childhood when they are still developing, in dementia when they have been lost, and in addiction where the forebrain is captured by other neural pathways reducing its ability to function. In these circumstances the more superficial level of behavioral learning may be particularly appropriate.

Higher forms of learning include vicarious learning. We can learn which country has poisonous snakes from a book or from local people. We do not need to learn this from direct experience. We can also use logic, reasoning and calculation to know that standing on tree branches of under a certain size will be dangerous. An interesting situation arises when there are too many complex factors and my computing power is overwhelmed. Here I can make an educated guess or use intuition.

Another form of learning is the unfolding of latent ability and knowledge. The ability to speak and use language is inherent in our nervous system and in our mind. But this ability does not manifest unless we experience others speaking, unless we are taught. Inner potential depends on having the right environment in which to unfold. Ironically, it is behaviorism, with its superficial approach,

32

which has shown us that the potential intelligence of animals is much greater than previously recognized. The same is true for man. Our consciousness contains tremendous potential which is unused because the environment is poor and education lacking.

BT can be used in complex problems as one part of a treatment plan. Marital problems are a good example. The causes and symptoms are probably multiple but specific problem behaviors may be well worth targeting. Making progress in one area can reduce hot spots of conflict and help rebuild a cooperative partnership to address the deeper problems. BT can be a starting point when the emotional temperature is so high and the past such a history of warfare that analysing emotional issues is initially impossible. A husband makes his wife's panic attacks worse by getting frustrated and angry that he cannot analyse and solve her problem. It may be best for him to agree just to hold and comfort her with no words or explanations. She will feel better and he will feel he is doing some good.

Connections to the Diversity of Life

BT is located on the Unified Field Chart in Chapter 1 at a superficial level of the mind. This is appropriate as it is characteristically aimed at individual outer behaviors. It was also developed from observations of very concrete external activity. However its knowledge links well and widely. The biologists can find the neuronal and chemical parallels to reward and learning. The effects of relaxation can be measured in the body

Behavioral principles can be found in the society column. Other people model good and bad behavior and give feedback for your actions. BT can also be used in deeper levels of the mind such as the cognitive realm by treating thoughts as behavior. In the transcending process of meditation more settled states of mind are found to be more rewarding. The most settled state is one of complete rest and a feeling of being at home with oneself. BT theory is a great example of basic laws which can be seen to be present at many levels of nature.

BT itself represents a very scientific approach to the mind. The principles of BT point in the direction of growth and unfolding of intelligence through direct experience. Behavior is sustained by reward. Once on the path of self development, our own experience of increasing benefits is the strongest motivator to continue.

Positive change is natural and driven by happiness

The general advice we gain from BT includes having a positive attitude; change and learning are easy and to be expected. We can be forward looking and not obsessed with past causes of illness or problems. The simplest advice from BT is to do what makes you happy. Happiness and reward drive growth and progress. Positive rewarding reinforcers are more effective than negative. Life can move forward in pursuit of more and more achievement. Even when negative reinforcement is needed, simply reducing a positive reward can be successful.

Achieve and recognise higher goals

When basic desires are met, there are higher goals to reach. This is especially true for man because our potential is so great. As we achieve goals we naturally look for higher goals from new and more profound reinforcers. In BT education is highlighted. We all want to educate our children well to fulfil their potential. We need to recognize that their potential, and our own as adults, is much greater than previously accepted.

BT sees learning and the growth of happiness as basic tend-encies. The ultimate goal of life is infinite happiness and increasingly rewarding types of fulfilment. The field of consciousness has an inherent ability to learn. It has an evolutionary tendency to grow which gives us creativity and the ability to generate new behavior. Consciousness can also understand the environment. The human mind can be aligned with the intelligence in our surroundings to make behavior more successful. For completely successful action our consciousness would need to be in harmony with all the intelligence underlying the environment. It would be in tune with the intelligence of nature.

34

Effectiveness of BT in Anxiety

BT is the treatment of choice for Specific Phobias with a very high cure rate. For Social Phobias BT is also strong especially where the problem is fairly specific such as public speaking. Similarly PTSD will respond if there is a fairly simple situation that you can re-expose yourself to such as driving a car after a traumatic car accident. Chronic general shyness may need help for underlying anxiety traits. For Agoraphobia BT is important but usually supplemented by Cognitive methods and by medication if very severe. For Panic Disorder, the cognitive aspect is even more important and again medication may be indicated if severe.

For Generalised Anxiety Disorder skills like relaxation are useful but complete cure harder than for Specific Phobias. We need to consider anxiety traits with meditation and life-style changes. Depression may need separate treatment with medication or psychological therapy if present.

Obsessional Compulsive Disorder has two aspects: obsessional thoughts and compulsive behaviors. Behavior Therapy is used for the compulsions but in combination with Cognitive Therapy and medication if the condition is severe.

Which people are comfortable with BT?

BT is suitable for a wide range of people as it is so simple. It is very useful for children, people with dementia, and adults with lower verbal or intellectual tendencies. However it is also good for people of normal intelligence. People with low confidence or hopelessness benefit from BT as they will feel they have achieved something for themselves. BT promotes your role as the Knower. It therefore appeals to people who want to learn and get control of their own problems.

Qualities of the mind identified in BT

∞ The mind has undeveloped potential and learns easily
∞ Relaxation and activity can be maintained together
∞ Knowledge is gained through experience
∞ Illness can have a basis in nonsense

∞ Chapter 3 ∞
Cognitive Therapy – Switching the Computer On

Thinking is a defining characteristic of human life. Our minds are forever filled with thoughts, especially if we are anxious. We strive to improve our thinking through education, knowing that more intelligent thoughts lead to more successful action. Yet our thoughts so often stray off task or into negative realms. No surprise that a therapy for thinking is so popular.

Cognitive Therapy (CT) has flourished in the latter part of the twentieth century and is now a major brand of psychological therapy. In public health services it is the market leader. Like Behavior Therapy, it is backed by strong scientific evidence from clinical trials, though its theoretical basis is not as clear as for BT. There are several schools or methods. Beck and Seligman are foundation thinkers and authors. However cognitive approaches are also evident in earlier texts. "As a man thinketh, so he is" is found in the Bible and was highlighted by James Allen in the title of his 1904 book.

CT uses our human ability to reflect on and manipulate our own thoughts (which sadly rats cannot do). This natural skill is one of those abilities we often forget to use, so we need to be taught. There are several different groups of strategies within CT.

Cognitive strategies

Firstly, thoughts can be treated as a form of behavior according to the principles of BT. Unwanted thoughts are identified and re-placed with healthier thoughts. New thoughts can be learned. This is the simplest level of CT. Anxiety is seen as caused by thinking too many anxious thoughts. Think more happy confident thoughts and you feel better. Not exactly rocket science, but this illustrates the principle that changing the content of consciousness changes our reality.

Secondly, we can use logic and reasoning to challenge false ideas. Thinking that "Flying is very dangerous" is a common phobic thought. If I can use logic to recognize this is not true, I travel more easily. Much of the work in CT has involved describing the many patterns and types of false thinking

Thirdly, the power of attention is used. We manipulate and redirect our focus of attention. This side of CT overlaps with techniques from hypnosis. Again we change the reality of experience by directly changing the focus and therefore the content of awareness.

Fourthly, there are wider methods, such as skills training and problem solving, which have strong cognitive elements. These often use behavioral strategies intermingled.

Thinking and feeling

The basis of CT for anxiety is that thought affects feeling. Anxious thoughts lead to or maintain an anxious and fearful mood. The reverse also seems to be true. In an anxious state you are more likely to over-estimate future risks and threats. So, vicious circles occur with thought and mood worsening each other. Whether or not cognition is a primary problem, thoughts and thinking patterns do serve to maintain anxiety. The original cause of anxiety may be less clear. But the success of CT shows that by improving cognitions anxiety does improve. There is also evidence that future relapse is less likely. This makes a good argument for cognitive processes being important in the causation of anxiety, even if cognition is not the only cause. On the brighter side, a confident mood and positive thoughts are also mutually self-supporting.

Anxious thoughts influence or determine your level of anxiety. Thoughts therefore need to be changed. The most characteristic approach of CT is the recognition of false thinking patterns. Many common patterns have now been documented and sometimes given great names such as "awfulizing". An extreme example is "catastrophic" thinking. In this, the catastrophic interpretations of experiences and situations are chosen. These occur particularly in panic disorder. You notice your heart rate has gone up, actually due to some trivial cause like exercise, but your interpretation is that you are

From Anxiety To Peace

having a heart attack and are about to die. A reality check is in order, from the knowledge of the nature of panic disorder and from memory of your own experiences of surviving prior panic attacks without cardiac disaster.

One general problem is lack of control and lack of feeling in control, with thoughts of helplessness. You feel unable to control your thoughts, or your feelings, let alone other people and outside events. CT allows you to regain control of your thinking. From there, feelings and actions can follow and you start to discriminate how much you can control the outside world. To control thoughts you must stand back from them. You must go to a deeper and more abstract level of your mind to view your surface thinking. You must also accept that your thoughts can be controlled by yourself. They are not determined solely by outside circumstances or events. Of course outside situations and people do provoke thoughts in my mind. But these thoughts are in my awareness. They come out of my consciousness. My interpretation of events, my reactions and conclusions are very much in my sphere of influence.

After a major trauma, memories of the event may themselves provoke anxiety. Simply tolerating having the thoughts in your mind may relieve this – just as exposing yourself to a phobic situation works in Behavior Therapy. Extreme traumas are dealt with differently by the brain, going more quickly through the amygdala nucleus and bypassing some of the normal memory processes. This allows for fast and energetic response. However it means some of the context of the event is not properly recorded. This leads to painful memories coming back for no clear reason and to inappropriate fears. Allowing yourself to remember in more detail will be painful but can help you to put the experience in its proper place and to move on.

The ability to stand back from thoughts and to go to a deeper level of our mind is crucial. This is transcending the surface level to a more abstract position. These deeper levels of consciousness are available to us but we forget to use them. If the mind is a computer, our thinking patterns and response patterns are the programs or software. By transcending to a deeper level we can reprogram the computer and install new software.

39

A course of CT

CT, like BT, is usually brief, typically eight sessions for anxiety. Again like BT, it is systematic and includes homework. The first step is identifying and observing your level of anxiety and your thoughts and in what circumstances these occur. This requires you immediately to stand back, to transcend the surface. Just this process of putting your attention on the problem is helpful and you become less bound up in the suffering.

The next step is identifying incorrect maladaptive thoughts and thinking patterns. These can then be challenged both by internal debate and discussion with your therapist. Then new thoughts are drawn up, often as verbal statements. Remember the 'Little Train Who Could', who verbalised as he chuffed up the hill " I think I can, I think I can". Generating new thoughts invokes your creativity and flexibility. These new thoughts are then practised.

The next level of abstraction is to find and practice new styles or patterns of thinking, not just individual thoughts. This could be catching your-self whenever black and white thinking occurs and applying shades of grey with more discrimination. Practice gives the experience to validate these steps of progress on the intellectual level.

Other techniques may be used, according to the type of problem and the particular school of CT. "Reframing" is a great tactic which has entered common parlance. Problems can be re-framed as challenges. Complaints about my business are now opportunities for me to improve it. Feelings themselves can also be relabelled. I suggested to a businessman who felt very anxious before any negotiation that this feeling might be better seen as arousal and mild aggression. He became quite a forceful negotiator.

In OCD you would learn to challenge irrational beliefs, reduce obsessional responses to anxiety and practice tolerance of anxiety. Extremely simple thinking techniques such as saying "Stop" to unwanted thoughts can be used.

The power of attention

Attention is the sentry or bouncer at the door to consciousness and can be very usefully directed. Distraction is the common method used. During panic or severe anxiety, attention is often captured by physical symptoms of palpitations, shaking, shortness of breath, or by catastrophic fearful thoughts. Distraction can be achieved by thinking more neutral thoughts. There is a phobia that is common but not much talked about, the fear of urinating in public toilets. For men this is more of a public performance. Anxiety about this makes it physically more difficult to start urinating, to relax those sphincters. Focusing attention on the problem makes it worse. Thinking of neutral topics such as baseball averages at this time has traditionally been found useful. Coincidentally, those same sporting averages can be usefully brought to mind in another situation to prevent premature ejaculation.

This may seem the same as replacing anxious thoughts with neutral ones. But rather than challenging the thoughts or finding opposite thoughts, this is simply taking attention away from them and from internal physical sensations. Another example is public speaking. If you concentrate on how much you are shaking and sweating you will not do well. Much better is to put your attention on the audience or on your prompt cards. Putting your attention on the here and now rather than on some dreaded future or dismal past is a part of mindfulness and of some more exotic psychotherapies like Gestalt.

Manipulation of attention is central to hypnosis and related methods such as Neuro-Linguistic Programming (NLP). Different senses can be used and thoughts manipulated. NLP looks at sensory styles of thinking. Do you tend to use the visual, auditory, or tactile style? Do you prefer learning by reading, hearing or using your hands? Use of the senses and attention together can be used to associate and dissociate things, as well as more cunning NLP manoeuvres.

Transcending beyond the surface of the mind

CT is accessible and popular because it is very positive and understandable. It has a most positive expectation, like BT, that we can improve and quickly. We have the ability to learn and the ability to observe and control our own mind. We can transcend the level of individual thoughts to reflect on them. We can transcend the patterns of thinking and reflect on the patterns. We can always go deeper in levels of abstraction. This identifies two crucial aspects of consciousness. Firstly, consciousness has this reflective nature of being able to step back and examine its own contents. Secondly, this going beyond or transcending is an extremely useful strategy.

Deeper levels are more comprehensive and positive

Cognitive therapy works because going beyond the surface means we are using more intelligent and more positive thinking which in turn maintains a more positive confident mood. The deeper we go the more comprehensive our thinking and the more useful.

Another encouraging and cheerful part of the CT perspective is that positive thinking is normal and healthy compared to the negative. Maladaptive thinking is logically incorrect, lacking discrimination or wider perspective. More profound and inclusive thinking will be more positive. Allowing our mind to use deeper levels of abstraction, deeper levels of consciousness, naturally results in more positive and appropriate cognition.

Caroline and the Cognitive Therapist

When Caroline sees the cognitive therapist, the approach and relationships are similar to that of Behavior Therapy. The CT method is explained and taught. There is recording in a diary and practice of new thinking as homework. The initial observation or recording focuses on thoughts before and during panic attacks which are then analysed. Catastrophic interpretation is found to be present. Caroline thinks the world is ending or at least her life or sanity is collapsing during an attack. This

42

interpretation is challenged logically by considering that previous attacks did not in fact lead to death or insanity. Knowledge of the nature of anxiety and panic is also used. Once panic sets in, the level of anxiety itself produces physical symptoms of the heart racing, shaking etc. So when these are experienced they can be attributed to just being part of anxiety.

Emphasising the patient as an instrument of knowing

The main focus in CT is on the thinking process in the patient, and the main tool used to discover this is the patient herself. This is a Knower to Knowing relationship as the therapist (Knower) encourages Caroline to be the method or process, Knowing, by which her thinking patterns, the Known, are observed.

Knower, Knowing and Known in Cognitive Therapy

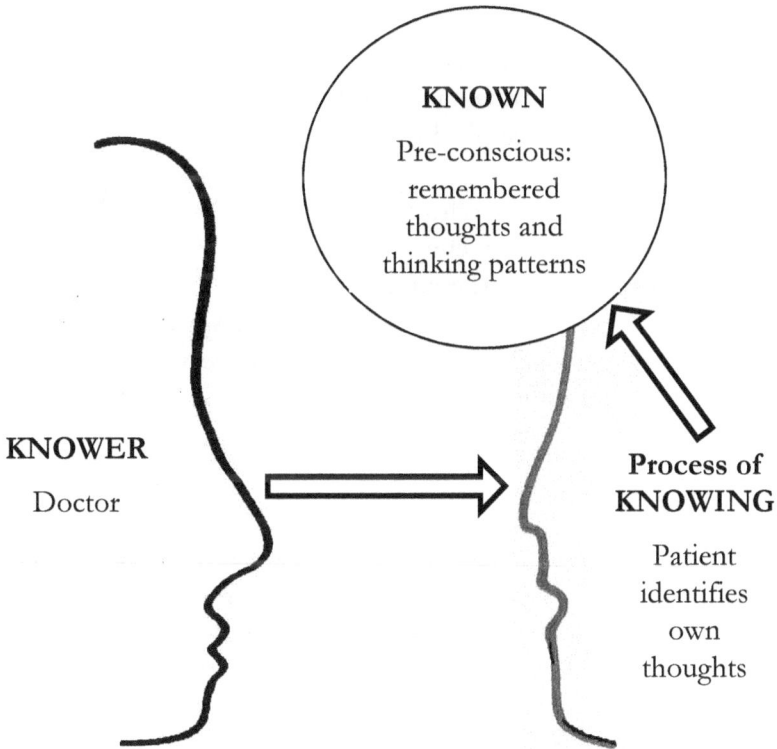

KNOWN

Pre-conscious:
remembered
thoughts and
thinking patterns

KNOWER

Doctor

**Process of
KNOWING**

Patient
identifies
own
thoughts

43

Cognitive Therapy

When Caroline is able to observe her own thinking patterns, the relationship changes to Caroline being the Knower. The therapist now provides a process or method, to which Caroline as Knower can come to know her own thinking patterns, the Known value. This configuration with the therapist as process of Knowing occurs more strongly in psychoanalytic therapy. In CT the process is easier because the object is Caroline's pre-conscious, not her unconscious. The pre-conscious is the area of the mind that is not in immediate current awareness but can fairly easily be accessed, like memories. When recording thoughts and looking for the patterns of thinking, these are quite easily retrieved and recorded in her homework.

As with BT, the patient should leave therapy with the ability to be Knower, Knowing and Known and so to be her own therapist. She contains the knowledge of CT in her own mind. This involves her having Knower, process of Knowing and Known all in her consciousness. As what is to be Known is her own thinking process, the Knower is at a deeper more abstract level. Her perspective has now transcended to a deeper level.

CT, as so far described, uses fairly basic intellectual and cognitive skills. Hence it can be applied to most people. No great intelligence is needed. Building on its outstanding success, CT is being developed or extended. Its use in psychosis is one example. CT is also extended to cover more complex emotional issues. Here it looks at more connections between different thoughts and feelings and patterns through time. Underlying beliefs or constructs are examined which may carry patterns of thinking through the years. These ideas are beginning to bridge the gap between the simple ideas of basic CT and the highly complex ideas of psychoanalysis.

Bypassing logic

Hypnosis is also related to CT, especially its techniques which use attention and association or disassociation. Hypnosis makes more use of imagination and the creativity of the mind. Dream-like tactics may be used such as metaphors. The blocks to solving a problem are circumvented by transposing to a metaphorical equivalent framework in which

From Anxiety To Peace

solutions are found. A man is anxious about his marriage. Repairing the relationship becomes rebuilding a house. Is it the foundations or the interior decorating that need attention? Does the house not have a heating system, or has he forgotten to stoke the fires?

There are different types of mental blocks, including emotional, cultural and cognitive. Thinking patterns may be stuck in a rigid state. To get through the surface logical and intellectual layers of the mind, hypnosis uses illogical tricks. Concentrating on a nonsensical statement can induce trance. "More is less" is an economical example. Hypnotic methods are also a part of normal communication. For good practitioners look no further than advertisers and politicians. Both want to persuade you to do something. "You cannot afford not to spend money on this product." And the simplest of old tricks are still the best. Cars are associated with attractive woman forming a basic association in men's minds. Zen training also includes the use of illogical ko'ans to get past not only the surface but all levels of the intellect. This is a brilliant but difficult path.

Hypnosis has had a place in therapy and an important part in the genesis of psychoanalysis. But it is a curious process pointedly described by Szasz as "Two people lying to each other". So why can it help? In a therapeutic situation, the hypnotist is trying to persuade the patient to get well. Of course the patient wants to get well. Why does he need help? Because he does not have access to his own imagination and his own creativity. The deeper levels of his mind are not open to him. The hypnotist's tricks provide some access though this will be limited to the specific areas addressed. Like BT, hypnosis is much better with a specific isolated symptom like a phobia. Success is very dependent on how hypnotisable you are.

Mindfulness techniques are increasingly popular. These come mainly from the Zen tradition and aim partly to promote a deeper quieter mind but more to teach better use of attention. This counteracts your perception and thinking being overshadowed and kicked around by emotions and outer activities. Mindfulness is used to create a stronger focus of attention and to allow more of your awareness to be engaged on important tasks.

Never forget your potential

We can learn from CT that change is not difficult. Remembering our simple intellectual abilities we can solve problems. Thinking patterns can be changed. Even personality problems which were previously judged to be untreatable can be helped. Do not accept problems as insurmountable and do not underestimate your own intelligence. Challenge anxious and negative thoughts just as we challenge unwanted behavior. Recognise magical thinking and the mirages of circular logic. We all own a state of the art computer between our ears and we must remember to keep it switched on.

The profession of Life Coaching has mushroomed. There is also money to be made from motivational speaking. The most educated and trained business people are seeking these external guides. Much of what they are buying is basic CT well packaged and with maximum positive spin: setting goals, prioritising, problem solving, positive thinking, and feedback. On-going coaching is mainly keeping you on task. This is a curious splitting of the mind, employing someone to repeatedly remind us of what we have already decided to do. Perhaps these speakers and coaches act as super role models and so borrow from Behavior Therapy as well, or is this a modern form of hypnotism?

Connections to the Diversity of Life

How does CT relate to the other areas on the Chart? It has a central role within the mental therapies because it is simple enough to link to BT and can be subtle enough to talk to psychoanalysis. Cognitive patterns which persist through time look similar to "complexes" seen in Psychoanalysis. With the power of new brain-scanning we are also starting to see the biological activity that parallels thinking processes. With computers becoming so dominant in human life CT has been given a huge boost as it is the psychological model closest to computer science. Ironically our increasing understanding of artificial intelligence is stimulating understanding of our own.

46

In Society, cognitive skills are taught in school to improve problem solving and resilience. Society uses cognitive processes to form norms of risk assessment. Our cognitive set greatly affects our view of the physical environment including risk.

Meditation uses the mind's ability to transcend to deeper levels. The deepest level is the most intelligent and creative.

Like Behaviorism, CT is very forward looking. Anxious emotions and thinking patterns are likely to relate to events of long ago. Do not waste time analysing these. Move on and focus on where you want to be in the future. Reprogram yourself and have a plan to maintain positive momentum. Prioritising can also allow you to let go unimportant problems. "Don't sweat the small stuff". Direct your attention and energy to where you most want to advance.

Education is the key to learning

We should continue our education throughout life and accumulate new skills. Do not assume because you are chronologically adult that you have learned all the skills even that most other people know, let alone the ones they could potentially achieve. The key lesson from CT is that the mind can transcend to make use of deeper levels. These levels are more abstract having wider intelligence, more creativity, and greater discrimination. From here thoughts are more powerful and more positive.

In practice CT is usually used with some elements from Behavior Therapy. Trying out new behaviors is used to confirm or consolidate changes in thinking patterns. This is referred to as Cognitive Behavior Therapy (CBT).

CT is the pre-eminent therapy of the waking state. It is a therapy of the intellect in its more surface values. CT uses transcending to other levels beneath the surface and it points to deeper levels. More development of consciousness is possible with more maturity and the full evolution of the intellect is within our grasp. Our intelligence and creativity can grow beyond previously accepted limits.

Evidence for CT in Anxiety

CT is an excellent therapy for the catastrophic thinking in Panic Disorder. It is combined well with BT in Agoraphobia and Social Phobia. It is not so important in Specific Phobias. Cognitive Therapy can be a part of treatment for Generalised Anxiety Disorder but other methods are needed where anxiety traits are prominent. Anxiety management programs typically use CT as just one element. Even combined with BT, CBT has only a 50-60% response rate. For Obsessional Compulsive Disorder CT is a major part of therapy for the obsessional thoughts but again is often not enough on its own. Drugs plus CT work better than CT alone.

When depression is also present, CT can also be directed against depressive thinking as CT is now one of the most evidenced therapies for depression. Another benefit of CT is that some of the strategies such as problem solving can be of use in other parts of your life.

CT is typically provided as individual therapy but can be found in groups, especially when part of a wider program including BT and relaxation for example. On-line CT is increasing in popularity and evidence accumulating for its effectiveness. On-line therapy can be completely therapist free or it can be used with coaching available when requested. This may be a stronger method allowing more flexibility in level of support.

Which people are comfortable with CT?

CT does not require a high level of intelligence but is easier for people used to abstract thinking. However developing the habit of abstract thought is very useful for people who do not usually use this ability. CT is very rewarding if you tend towards helplessness and lack of the Knower role. Obviously CT is a good choice if you are already aware of being stuck in bad thinking patterns.

From Anxiety To Peace

Qualities of the mind identified in CT

∞ The mind has abstract levels below the surface thinking level
∞ Our attention can easily transcend to these deeper levels
∞ Deeper levels are more intelligent
∞ Deeper levels support confident positive mood
∞ Knowledge and experience complement each other in progress

∞ Chapter 4 ∞
Psychoanalysis – Enquiring Within

The archetypal image of a psychiatrist is that of the psychoanalyst, making bizarre interpretations of a sexual nature in a mid-European accent. Ideas from Psychoanalysis have become part of modern culture. We all know about neuroses, defences and phallic symbols. Anxiety is a core feature of neurosis. Even though very few of us have actually been in analysis, its concepts have been a major force in shaping our society.

Psychoanalysis dominated Western psychiatry during the middle of the twentieth century. The original and true Freudian analysis would take five sessions a week for several years, a huge investment. Analysis based therapy developed as a less intense watered down version being delivered usually once a week. The ideas of Psychoanalysis have been accepted in many other academic disciplines. This intellectual achievement has been greater than the actual success of Psychoanalysis in individual treatment, which has been quite modest. In the age of evidence-based medicine, analysis became sadly known as the scientifically proven method of earning a living, being less proven as an effective treatment.

Freud himself was a very scientific man and took concepts from classical 17th-century physics plus the rapidly developing science of chemistry. From this he borrowed reactions and transformations to apply to emotions in his science of mind. Anxiety related to work might transform to anger directed to family at home. The European gentleman in the late nineteenth century also knew of archaeology and mineralogy. To find older treasures, to unearth the past, you need to dig deeper. If current problems have their causes in the past, then to discover their true meaning, you must delve beneath the surface of your mind.

51

Sadly, the late nineteenth century was also the time of some very negative philosophies. Was the man's nature not in fact naturally noble and good? The philosophy which Freud developed had a strong negative slant. He came to see life as an uneasy compromise between the baser demands of the body and the higher restrictions of society. The model he constructed came from the study of illness and imbalance where conflicts are emphasised.

Despite this, many of Freud's ideas have validity and lasting value, including some of his basic observations. He saw different parts to the mind whose interactions reflected outside relationships. The inner world is dynamic, and its relationships are paralleled in our outer reality.

Anxiety in general is seen by analysts as a less honest or genuine emotion than depression. An analyst once told me that, "When a client weeps, I rejoice". Anxiety may mask underlying depression. Panic and feeling unsafe could be related to a fairly obvious prior life event such as the death of a parent. This loss evokes childhood fears as much as the absence of a current support. Sexuality is a common suspect in analytical causes. Freud suggested Agoraphobia, the fear of being out and about in public, might reflect fear of being pointed out as someone who had had incestuous sexual relations. Whether such incest, or sexual abuse, has occurred in reality or just in fantasy has been a fluctuating debate. Unlikely and fanciful maybe, but tragically for many societies, the frequency of undeniably real sexual abuse is still high. The few patients of mine who reported apparently happy consensual adult incest have all had panic attacks.

Freud is criticised for his obsession with sex. His core concept of libido is in fact wider than just sexuality but certainly he paid much less attention to other positive forces or felt they were less important. He lived in a society of sexual restrictions and no doubt of sexual frustrations. Even though many of us now live in very permissive societies, sex is still a dominant concern and over emphasised in relationships. Society still does not have its sexual life in satisfactory shape and is stuck, blocked from pursuing other goals. Social instability and cultural uncertainty make the rules of sexual interaction

52

trickier. Other positive feelings such as love, altruism, and responsibility, have become less easy.

Most schools developing from Freud's work looked for more positive philosophies and better outcomes. Jung found more value in spirituality, which Freud tended to dismiss. Kohut looked for the "Restoration of the Self" with more optimism about our control over our mental life. Humanist schools in general went to a more positive view of other people and a greater capacity for personal growth.

Discovering the unconscious

Freud identified the importance of the unconscious mind. As the causes and meaning of illness were not apparent to the patient's conscious surface awareness some digging was needed. Freud demonstrated the existence of the unconscious also by inference from other phenomena such as jokes, from mistakes or slips, and of course from dreams. Freud's best writing is about dreams and the communication between the waking state and the dreaming state of consciousness. Freud was preoccupied with the role of dreams and the unconscious. Of course in an affluent society, we can now pay others to dream for us. Films are the collective dreams of our time.

A woman with anxiety had learned from her childhood to be quiet and submissive if she wanted help and protection. In time she married a strong, loud and assertive fireman. But she dreamed of herself rescuing her son from fire. In her dreams she was as she wanted to be, more active and more competent. Freud recognized that knowledge must be lively in the patient to have power. Having the dream is not enough. She must come to know for herself, when awake, the dream's meaning. She must gain insight. Knowledge is only meaningful and potent when integrated in her awareness or waking consciousness.

Freud believed that thought and feeling could be integrated better from knowledge of the unconscious. Gaining self knowledge could be achieved by becoming aware of what was previously hidden, buried, and unconscious. "Freudian slips" became part of everyday language showing that we have accepted the unconscious exists.

When we repeatedly forget to phone someone, this hidden part of our mind is blocking the call. There is some reason not to call. We cannot easily say if this is a valid and useful reason or some spurious negative feeling from the past no longer relevant. We need to bring the block into consciousness so it can be evaluated and integrated with our conscious reasons for making the call.

Looking inwards

In an era when social extroversion is celebrated, introspection is not so fashionable. Although Freud recommended self knowledge, he judged that too much attention being directed inwards, too much pleasure from playing with your own inner workings, was unhealthy, even perverted. Jung had a more positive spin on inner attention or narcissism. By looking inside we can find "creative imagination" in the depths of consciousness. Here new energy, new answers, and inspiration can be found.

Jung was a more spiritual man and saw many superficial problems, especially in middle and later life, being caused by spiritual questions and uncertainties. He believed personality could grow and achieve spiritual peace.

Jung's description of the collective unconscious was another step beyond Freud's limit. He greatly expanded the scope of consciousness across space and time. Myths and archetypes have their universality across cultures and also through the ages of time. Archetypal roles can be seen as different frequencies or wave-forms that are supported in the sea of consciousness. Carol Pearson popularised some of Jung's ideas in her book "The Hero Within". She suggests society is moving from a time when the Warrior archetype dominates to the time of the Magician. The Warrior battles to prove his worth. The Magician can transform life to make the world he wants. He uses the skill of envisioning a desired future in order to create it.

Kohut also had very positive views on narcissism. Inner attention can open the doors to creativity, empathy, wisdom and humour. He wrote of the Analysis of Self and Restoration of Self. Like Jung he found the inner and deeper levels of the mind important and useful

54

for individual growth. The Ego schools use self to mean that individual experience of self, not an expanded unbounded experience of transcendental Self. In Freud's work, the ego is but one of many actors in the play of the mind. It may have a relatively weak part, trying to compromise between the more educated super ego and the primitive id. Ego schools do take a more positive view. There is more room for free will, more ego strength and sense of the self available. Other people are also seen much more positively. Interpersonal communication serves to validate our own experience of self.

Relationships

Psychoanalysis is conducted through the analyst patient relationship. This can become intense and intimate enough to essentially re-enact the patient's original parenting. But this takes a very long time. Huge dependency on the analyst is built up to create trust and allow safe exploration of problems within the therapeutic relationship. Past problems are transferred into this therapeutic experience. The ending of an analysis, the termination of therapy, is difficult and painful because the relationship has been so intense and valuable. But this separation is crucial, just as separation from parents is crucial to maturing into an adult. In a poor analytic therapy there may be no end. The relationship and dependency just continue. Separation and individuation can safely occur and loss can be tolerated when the integration or balance in the therapeutic relationship is transferred back into the patient's own internal world.

"Object relations" is a marvellous name for an influential school of analytic therapy. Objects here are in fact usually people, represented in the patient's mind. Separation is the main concern of the school. How does the infant separate from its mother? Is the mother a good object, a bad one, or both? Again, depression or the depressive position is more valid then anxiety. The sadness of separation and the deficiencies in the maternal object are a reality to be accepted. However this is still a fairly optimistic school. Mothers do not have to be perfect and separation can be survived OK. The correspondence between the internal and external relationships is also a central theme.

Humanist therapies, even more than the ego schools, have positive ideas about other people and emphasise our potential for growth. Rogers brilliantly summarised the personal specifications of the good therapist as: (1) being genuine and honest (2) having the capacity for accurate empathy (3) maintaining an unconditional positive regard for others. This famous triad owes a little to Dale Carnegie's advice to give honest and sincere appreciation in order to "Win friends and influence people". Rogers' criteria are hard to truly measure up to unless you are enlightened – the three criteria relating easily to the Knower, Knowing and Known aspects.

There is a galaxy of related therapies often called psychodynamic or just dynamic therapies. Some try to increase communication and connection between people by breaking down the barriers that separate them. Encounter groups used non-directive acceptance to encourage mental, emotional and physical contact. Gestalt, a more sophisticated therapy, reduces the blocks to awareness of the here and now, to increase the sense of wholeness. Multiple perspectives are used and playing with different senses in an effort to expand awareness. In a dream analysis you could look at each person in the dream as usefully representing an aspect of yourself. They may simultaneously represent other people – illustrating the efficient intelligence of dream processes.

Self Realisation

Another important development has been schools advocating Self realisation as a goal of therapy. Maslow was a primary developer of these ideas, though his school of therapy did not become large in itself. He showed there was a hierarchy of goals or needs. As basic needs, such as safety, physical comfort, food etc. are met we become able to aspire to higher goals such as social achievements. The highest goal is Self realisation, the full development of conscious experience. This is knowledge of our own transcendental nature. Maslow reported these experiences as occurring and being keenly sought by people who had them. But he did not have a good technique for achieving this transcendental experience. This explains why his work is more descriptive and aspirational than it is therapeutic.

One interesting difference in Maslow's approach from Freud's is that for Maslow anxiety could be better than depression. Going forward involves anxiety about being able to do more, to accomplish new goals. Starting in senior school provokes anxiety. But it is clearly a necessary step and a step up to the next level of childhood. Going backwards or staying stuck at one level would be depressing. Freudian analysis has a very past directed approach and this is why depression is favoured and future growth under-estimated.

More modern dynamic theories were developed to find more optimistic and briefer therapies. Only the highly motivated and wealthy can see an expensive analyst five times a week. Another driver has been to simplify Freud's ideas which became intellectually too complex, adding to the emotional barriers to understanding. Transactional Analysis is a popular derivative approach suggesting Parent, Adult, and Child roles which reflect some of the values of super ego, ego, and id.

Many briefer therapies include some analytic ideas. However there are dangers in cutting Psychoanalysis down to size. Firstly the briefer time may prevent sufficiently strong therapist-patient relationships. One of the central planks of the analytic method is working directly in the "transference", the transference of problems into the therapist-patient relationship. The second risk is that knowledge stays with the therapist. The therapist may see clear interpretations quickly and be able to spell these out. But they may not be discovered or owned by the patient. At its worst this becomes psycho-babble, sounding good but having little useful effect. Counselling may drift into this hazardous swamp. Vague and supportive counselling is often enjoyed by clients and councillors are well intentioned, but there is surprisingly little evidence that it works. Recovery is unlikely to be faster from temporary life setbacks and recovery from more complex traumas takes more than this. Focused counselling has a clearer place, where some external knowledge and guidance is useful, as in career counselling.

Such is the desire for outside assistance that counselling is a growth industry of our age. Some of the most popular types of counselling, such as marital counselling, have the least evidence to support them. There is a great desire for knowledge and growth but we are looking in the wrong places.

The internal dynamics of the mind

Regardless of its varied clinical success, the analytical schools made several important discoveries. They found that there is much more to conscious life than its surface values and that the mind has rich internal processes. These inner dynamics have been caused by past experience and in the present they shape outside relationships and our view of external reality. Lack of support in childhood leads to an anxious adult who then looks for a protective and strong partner. As in Cognitive Therapy, the world is as we are, as we think it is. But in analysis this extends beyond the colouring of mood and thinking patterns. The pattern of our relationships also reflects our internal unconscious mental structure.

Beth was a successful young woman in her late twenties who had become a hard-working project manager. She was also successful at hiding from her colleagues that she had high levels of anxiety, with self doubt, obsessional absurd thoughts and feelings of worthlessness. These prevented her from having close relationships. As a young child she had been sexually abused by her father and she had always blamed herself for this and had not been able to talk to anyone about this. Medication had little effect and simple Cognitive Therapy was only partially helpful. It did give her enough confidence to talk about her past. She was then able to engage in a trusting therapeutic relationship and process her childhood emotions. This freed her from the grip of inappropriate guilt and put the past behind her. Her anxieties then relented leaving her free to enjoy her busy work life and to develop a new loving relationship.

Self Knowledge

Another central principle of analysis is that of self knowledge. This is the key to growth and recovery. Later schools are more positive about

58

growth, because they are more positive about the deeper contents on the mind. Self knowledge involves ownership of knowledge, insight requiring both knowledge and experience.

The therapeutic relationship is all

Lastly the importance of the doctor-patient relationship is emphasised far beyond that needed for Behavior Therapy or Cognitive Therapy. One consequence of this is that the analyst himself should be as balanced and healthy as possible. An analyst should know himself through his own analysis. The work of analysis has to take place within the therapeutic relationship. This has to be strong and it has to be lively with intelligence.

What can we learn about the mind from Psychoanalysis? There are many parts to mental experience, many particles within the whole personality. These interact with each other. This implies there must be a medium or field in which these parts and dynamics all exist. This has to be the field of consciousness. Even the unconscious is really a different mode of functioning of this field, just one that communicates poorly with the waking state of consciousness. Analysis clearly discovered that there is more to the mind than the ordinary waking state. Deeper levels do exist. These include the individual unconscious and the collective unconscious. The collective unconscious transcends time as well as individuality. More modern schools have identified the Self as having not just an ego role but also a transcendental nature. The basis of the personality is this transcendental Self.

Caroline and the Psychoanalyst

When Caroline visits the analyst she has a very different experience. There is little or no explanation of the process. The session may start with silence to give every chance for Caroline's emotions and her unconscious to speak. The analyst does not ask a series of questions about Agoraphobia or panic attacks, even if these are known to be her main complaint. A therapeutic space is created between the analyst and Caroline for her to fill however she wishes. She may find or choose some quite different underlying issues to her presenting symptoms. Only later does the analyst suggest interpretations to guide her progress and these will be checked with her for validation. Traditional methods such as asking her to recall a dream serve to encourage the expression of unconscious material. Simply lying down on a couch encourages her to change her state of mind and modes of communication.

Forcing the patient into the position of the Knower

The analyst does not reveal anything about himself. He refuses to be an example or model. He does not want to be an object and avoids this position. He also avoids the Knower role, not asking many questions or giving out conclusions or advice. He resolutely stays in the process role supporting Caroline's gaining self knowledge. The analyst and his relationship becomes the process through which Caroline, as Knower, can see herself and learn about herself. The part of her mind she is guided towards is her unconscious, that which by definition she does not currently know. Analytic therapy may be called "process" psychotherapy. The analyst acts like a slow interpreter, mediating a conversation between Caroline in her waking state and the unconscious levels of her mind. This may seem a bizarre conversation, even ridiculous by everyday standards. Caroline says that during panic she feels anxious, unsafe, and afraid of losing control. The analyst asks if she fears losing control of her aggression and killing someone. This strange suggestion may make sense in the language of the unconscious. Or is she afraid of losing control sexually and having an orgasm? In the unconscious context this could be meaningful even though it may seem absurd to her waking mind. Even complete silence can be interpreted. This is a beautiful contribution of analysis, finding meaning and knowledge even in silence, sensing the dynamic vibrations in silent awareness.

As a new patient you find the analytic process uncomfortable. This shows how much we expect a therapist to be an expert and provide answers. We do not expect to have to find the answers for ourselves, let alone in ourselves. In the world of scientific knowledge we have given up the position of the Knower to the experts.

Knower, Knowing and Known in Psychoanalysis

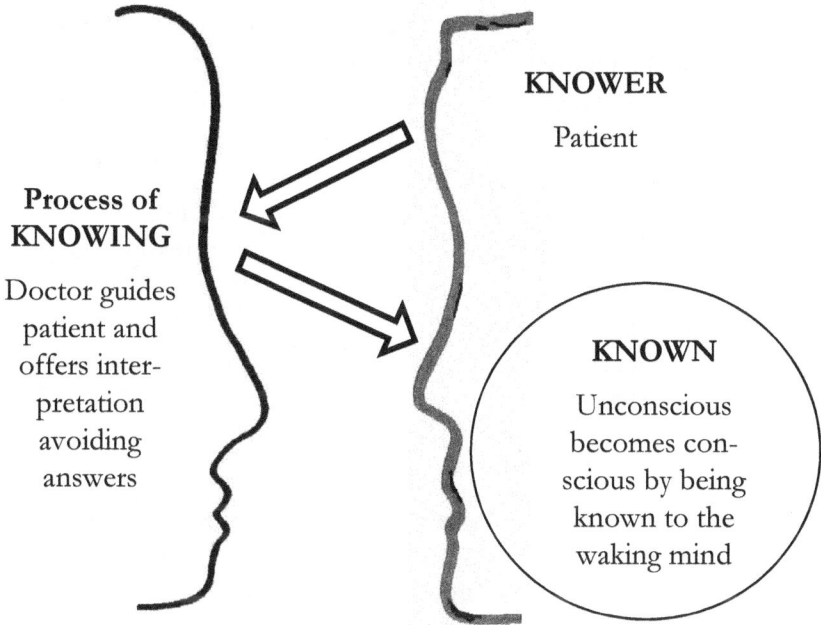

KNOWER

Patient

Process of KNOWING

Doctor guides patient and offers inter- pretation avoiding answers

KNOWN

Unconscious becomes con- scious by being known to the waking mind

Freud's brilliance saw that both the Known and Knowing values of knowledge were very different in different levels of the mind. The unconscious uses a different language and uses different logic to our waking state. This makes the task of being a Knower of this knowledge even more challenging.

By not revealing his own personality and avoiding the Known role, the therapist is a blank screen onto which Caroline can project images from her own internal world. Past relationships can then be transferred into the therapeutic relationship. The analyst does then pick up the position of Known, but in a special role which is scripted by Caroline's unconscious. He does this to facilitate an internal dialogue played out on the therapeutic stage.

Working in the transference, as it is called, allows the patient to relive the past. Powerful memories can be revealed in this way. Past relationships and conflicts can be re-enacted to give insight and to enable the patient to rehearse them differently. If separation from mother led to excess anxiety, the analyst's being away on holiday will cause similar stress. The analytic view of personal history is that it is a spiral or helix. The pattern of relationships and events repeats itself over and over through time and the stages of life. Fear of criticism in childhood persists into adult life and leads to choosing a job below your abilities so you can be sure that you do it well. The pattern of fear is carried in the mind and inner conflicts. These will then be projected or transferred into the therapeutic relationship. The patient feels criticised by the therapist or is critical towards him. If the patient can learn, for example, that a close caring relationship is possible in therapy without abuse, they can change and move on, breaking the cycle.

Beyond the Unconscious

Analysis is a path of self discovery and considers self knowledge most valuable. Analysis advises us not to get stuck in conflict. If the past is unresolved we can work through this. Growth and progress are possible if slow. But despite being a school of depth psychology, Freudian analysis does not have enough to say about the ultimate or higher goals of man and society.

The analytic schools do allow the mind to go beneath the surface. They borrow from hypnosis some illogical methods to sneak past the intellect on guard. They also strive to resolve thoughts and feelings piece by piece and through slow reintegration create layers of increasing wholeness. It is the complexity of the mind that makes this a long and difficult journey.

Connections to the Diversity of Life

Analysis is a depth psychotherapy. It sits at a lower level of the mind. It has been rather self-contained, not connecting well to the models of biology despite the importance it gives to physical drives. Nor does it relate well to more simple minded behavioral and cognitive theories. This failure to connect is a major reason why our modern model of the mind is poorly integrated within itself. Meaningful connections to deeper aspects of society such as religion are similarly poor. Psychoanalysis has been blamed for enabling a culture of Moral Relativism. It has better relations with the Arts and influenced how these are interpreted.

Analysis has been an important description of internal layers of the mind. It has shown us that the mind does have depths to be explored. Consciousness can be expanded and intuitive knowledge found. Analysis to its credit is still developing and many of its principles have endured as important signposts to the inner world. Analytic work has shown the mind to be deeper, richer, and self-interacting. But it has been better at describing the past than the future. It now needs to move on from the world of 19th century science for the force of evolution towards self knowledge to overcome the blocks of the past.

The ideas of analysis are fascinating but have not yet been successful in plumbing the ultimate depths of consciousness. Analysis understands that the inner world is the basis of the outer world and through self knowledge we can create a better inner world. Sadly the analytical path to self knowledge turned out to be a most difficult journey. On the foundation of analysis, modern schools have become more positive and more expansive.

The central advice from analysis is not to settle for a life stuck at one level, fixated at a point where conflicts have not been resolved. Seek self knowledge. The positive drive towards personal growth and integration is powerful. Our obsession with individuality may have hampered our search for deeper levels of experience. We do not easily let go of our individual egos. But enlightenment will be seen to be an expansion of individual life not a negation. As Tennyson wrote: "The loss of personality (if so it were) seeming no extinction but the only true life." Psychoanalysis was handicapped by starting from the examination and description of illness and ignorance. It has been on a slow journey from there towards discovering enlightenment. The

63

extra element of how to gain transcendent consciousness has been elusive.

Evidence for Psychoanalysis in Anxiety

Psychoanalysis does not see superficial diagnoses as important so it is hard to assess the evidence as we can for some other therapies. Trials of brief analytical therapy for specific disorders such as Generalised Anxiety have not been successful. Full traditional psychoanalysis is beyond the reach of most people for practical and financial reasons. Less intense dynamic therapies do have a place but it is harder to predict when they will work. They may be indicated where there are emotional or relationship problems that seem to predate the anxiety disorder. Individual symptoms, especially in OCD, may be seen as having unconscious or symbolic meaning and worked with in this way. Though not the first choice of therapy, dynamic therapy is also more indicated where there has been known past trauma such as childhood abuse. However you may need to do some work in BT and CT to learn how to tolerate distress before undertaking an analysis based therapy where you do need to be able to cope with emotional pain.

Which people are comfortable with Psychoanalysis?

Very few are in a position to have a full five days a week analysis because of time and money constraints. Any insight or process psycho-therapy demands a commitment not just of time and money but also of mental and emotional effort. It takes work. To cope with the emotional demands of analytic therapy it is best to have some current supports otherwise you become too dependent on the therapist. Wanting to know more about yourself is a must but do not expect answers to be simply given to you.

As with CT, analytic therapy is easier for people who have some psychological awareness. However, it can also be very beneficial for some-one who has not used their potential in the process of Know-ing. Analysis is mostly an emotional approach so not so easy for people who are too dependent on logic and factual knowledge.

From Anxiety To Peace

Qualities of the mind identified in Analysis

∞ Self knowledge and integration of parts of the mind leads to
  health
∞ There are distinct states of consciousness: waking,
  dreaming and sleeping which all have their own realities
∞ There is a level of consciousness beyond the individual:
  collective consciousness

∞ Chapter 5 ∞
Biological Psychiatry – A Solid Scientific Frame

In an age of science we have invested our money and our hopes into biological medicine. This is the dominant paradigm in psychiatry today. Couches have been replaced by MRI scanners.

Biological drug therapy is powerful in the short-term relief of severe anxiety symptoms. However it has been less effective in milder illness and in treating underlying causes. Indeed the basic cause of anxiety disorders remains unclear in the biological model. It is obvious that some individuals and families are worriers, nervous or prone to anxiety. We do not yet know the exact chemical basis for this.

Discovering the finer intelligence of the body

The scientific method has been applied to the human body especially in the last 200 years. With increasingly fine microscopes, we can now see down through the levels of organs, tissues and cells to the molecular level. We see objectively finer and finer levels of structure. The model of the body that emerges from this scientific process is one of layers. At each level we have studied the functioning and know how the body works at deeper levels of biological intelligence.

In the 1950's and 1960's the main classes of psychoactive drugs were discovered. That is to say the modern therapeutic classes of drugs were discovered. Recreational and addictive mind-bending substances have been known for centuries. Some drugs have been so successful and so widely used that the brand leaders have become household names, Prozac and Valium being the prime examples. Indeed these drugs have been so extensively used that many household medicine cabinets have a supply.

It would be nice to think that science first came to understand the chemical level of the brain, was then able to determine which chemicals would be therapeutic and then developed these as medicines. Strangely, the exact opposite has happened. Benzo-diazepine drugs like Valium were found to reduce anxiety and we therefore concluded the brain has benzodiazepine receptors Then we looked for the natural chemicals in the body that bind to these sites. One of the nicest examples is a chemical in mother's milk. Another reason for not using formula.

An underlying assertion in biological psychiatry is that changes in the physiology lead to changes in subjective experience. This is certainly true. It is the very reason why people drink alcohol and take other mind altering drugs. The change in the chemistry of the brain does lead to changed experience. But the opposite is also true. Psychological change leads to physical changes. If a terrorist walks into your office with a bomb, your subjective reaction leads to a clear physical change, adrenaline mobilising your body for action. It is only recently that we have had fine enough brain scanning and other techniques to see brain functioning change in real-time with different experiences. We are therefore at a crucial time as we start to demon-strate that psychological methods can lead to functional changes. No longer can the biologist automatically trump the psychological and social therapists by claiming biological changes take precedence. Cognitive Behavioral Therapy is known to be effective as medication in many forms of anxiety. It will be fascinating to see how their effects on brain functioning are similar or different.

We are now down to the genetic level of life. This will eventually reveal the genes that predispose to anxiety disorders and most are likely to be polygenic rather than simple. We do not yet know if this will lead to new or better drug treatments or whether therapy at the genetic level will be practical and safe for disorders of the brain. Scientists are hopeful and others of us are fearful as well.

Uncertain progress

A curious feature of the chemical approach to mental illness is that since the 1950's and 60's this approach has received most of the research funding, but it has not made great advances in terms of

68

therapy. This is particularly true in the anxiety states. The main advance has been the recognition that many anti-depressant drugs work in anxiety and that panic disorder responds differently to generalised anxiety. Anti-depressants are much less addictive than benzodiazepines but do have a worse side-effect list. We still wait for another break-through and genetics is promising to deliver, but there are no guarantees here. The very large investment in drugs and chemical research has not in fact delivered a great deal new in the last 40 years for those with anxiety.

Anti-anxiety drugs have a problematic history as they were over-used and led to a generation of addicted patients. Their use has been cut back but they remain a powerful short-term strategy to reduce anxiety. The story of their overuse is interesting. Valium and its relatives became overused and came to be seen as an emotional prop for people who were addicted. Once a sufficiently large number of people were taking these drugs this practice became unacceptable. It is quite acceptable for someone with diabetes to take insulin for the rest of their life. But it is not acceptable for someone with anxiety or social stress to take Valium indefinitely. This is not just because the drug becomes less effective over time as this is not always true. It is because society fundamentally does not believe it is right for relatively common stresses to be handled in this way. So in the case of Valium and the benzodiazepines society intervened in the individual doctor-patient transactions.

Depression provides a definite contrast to anxiety in this regard. Depression has been successfully sold as an illness in contrast to anxiety which many see as more of a personality weakness. Life-long Valium for anxiety was voted out by the public as much as by doctors. But we now have an increasing number of patients on antidepressant drugs for years or indefinitely. Only time will tell whether this also will be seen as unacceptable.

Politically, the biologists have conquered the analysts. The major training programmes which were dominated by analysis are now in biological hands. The brainless has been replaced with the mindless. This battle has been fairly bloodless as the analysts had so little ammunition. In the USA, some famous court cases have underlined

69

the rights of patients to at least be informed about well-evidenced treatments. This favours biological and cognitive treatments where short-term research has been especially strong.

Most biological psychiatrists do describe themselves as eclectic or bio-psycho-social and many would provide their drug therapy in the context of other approaches. Financial pressures do favour drugs in the short term. Many patients would prefer to have CBT for anxiety rather than drugs. But while I can prescribe a drug in moments, CBT takes a number of longer sessions. The benefits of psychosocial intervention may be much longer term and so are harder to demonstrate then the relief of symptoms in a few weeks.

Biological intelligence

Science has travelled down to the level of DNA, our genetic base. DNA is now seen as more active and interactive than previously. It is not just a blueprint to be rolled up and put away after the body is built. It remains an active level of biological intelligence involved in the on-going process of determining which elements of the body are produced and emphasised. The body is very complex at every level and this is especially evident at the chemical level, the level of individual molecules. Genes relate to individual proteins which in turn handle other molecules. All of these then interact giving rise to many possible relationships and interconnections.

In the central nervous system each neuron has their branches or dendrites spreading out to many others, up to 20,000 others for the well-connected neurone. Then there are dozens of neuro-transmitter molecules that are sent out from one neuron to talk to receptors on the neighbouring neurone. One neuro-transmitter may be involved with many different pathways in different areas of the brain. It is the vast number of interconnections that support the brain's huge intelligence. Drugs are typically designed to interact with one neuro-transmitter. This has been cynically likened to attempting to talk to somebody but only using one word. Most mental illnesses are clearly not due to a simple imbalance in one neuro-transmitter.

A central problem for medicines is that even the successful ones generally only work for about 70 per cent of patients. We have little idea who will respond to a specific drug and use trial and error. Genetics may provide more answers but again there are no guarantees. These individual differences are poorly understood by modern science.

So we await genes. Almost certainly we shall be able to determine who has which genes making them susceptible to which illnesses. But this may not lead to new cures or even prevention. Biologists may find themselves embarrassed to be in the same boat as the analysts, having great descriptive knowledge but knowledge which has limited therapeutic value.

In the meantime we should not be sitting idly round. For example, it is clear that some of us are far more susceptible to the effects of caffeine than others. No doubt there is some genetic basis for this. We do not need to wait till the gene or genes are identified. We can easily test ourselves. Does coffee in the evening result in you going to sleep later? If you have any tendency to anxiety, does coffee make you more likely to feel anxious or even have a panic attack? If you drink coffee regularly, try stopping. If you experience head-aches and irritability then you are more addicted than you might have thought. In this case you will feel better without it but you need to give it some time for the effects of withdrawal to dissipate.

Minor mental imbalance and self medication

We cannot yet see physical imbalances in the commoner minor mental problems. Minor imbalance or stress are the signs we usually experience first. Subjective awareness that something is out of kilter occurs well before anything gross can be seen by someone else. In the office of the family doctor in primary care, many people complain of non-specific symptoms – general tension and tiredness are popular. Yet no physical illness can be found. Examination and tests are normal. There are fashions in how we categorise these vague states of dis-ease. They may be attributed to a virus, or blood sugar, or the liver, or nerves and stress. Individual countries have their own favourites. If the subjective

71

experience is of discomfort, there is a corresponding physiological imbalance but it is too subtle to see with the methods of Western medicine. This is a great shame as early imbalance need to be detected and dealt to if we are to prevent illness from developing.

If imbalances in normal functioning persist we start being tempted to treat them as illnesses. There is argument as to what constitutes an illness and so merits treatment especially in the world of mental health. Is shyness really mild Social Phobia that should be treated or is it your nature to be shy?

While symptoms may be identifiable - social anxiety, poor sleep or minor mood disturbance - it is less clear how and when to treat. Even if drugs are acceptable, their effects are often short-term and no use once stopped. There is a growing belief in the population that we should attend more to our lifestyles. To improve mild anxiety or to improve sleep we should live differently rather than depend on medicine. Paradoxically, at the same time we are taking more and more psychoactive medicine and expecting treatment for milder states of distress. We are ambivalent, or is this hypocrisy? Perhaps in matters of the mind we feel too helpless, not believing we can really change ourselves.

The same ambivalence is found in our use of illegal and legal recreational drugs. Alcohol, cannabis and more exotic drugs demonstrate the power and the complexity of the brain. You feel more relaxed but you also pay the penalty. Alcohol remains a major factor in so many physical illnesses. The rate of liver disease in the population is like a national diagnostic marker for a country's alcoholism. Alcohol's effect on mental health is terrible, worsening anxiety on the rebound, precipitating psychosis and depression, even suicide. Yet alcohol is legal and apparently enjoyed by many. That is perhaps the saddest aspect. Many people find it hard to enjoy themselves if they are not under the influence of alcohol. We naturally desire to be happy and will risk the damage of alcohol and drugs for the temporary changes they bring to our state of consciousness.

Most of us are not main-lining heroine, smoking dope or drinking hugely more alcohol than the government advises. But are we using coffee to start up in the morning, paracetamol to cope with the

72

stress headaches at work and just a couple of drinks to unwind in the evening? Even these are all pointers to an internal chemistry not coping with life to our satisfaction. All these props, minor and major, are signals of our stress levels.

One curious aspect of medication and illegal drugs is that they often have an effect on disturbed mental state regardless of the cause of that disturbance. Anxiety may be due to physical illness, social circumstances and events, your style of thinking or complex emotional dynamics. But drugs will probably have some effect. This may be dangerous in that drugs can be used to help you tolerate situations that should not be tolerated. Alcohol or Valium may help you tolerate being abused by a husband who you are ambivalent about leaving. But used appropriately, medication can help in the short term giving you enough energy and enough concentration to start changing the situation causing the stress or to start changing your thinking patterns.

Martin had severe panic and social phobia in his twenties but made a good marriage and did well in his career becoming more confident. However he continued to take benzodiazapines when under stress. A period of family conflict in his early sixties bought the panic back. Even when the family settled down he remained anxious and developed secondary depression. He started on an anti-depressant and became well enough to taper off the benzodiazapines. Unfortunately he suffered from sexual side-effects, the last thing he wanted at that time. A change to another type of anti-depressant solved this problem and he remained well. How long he should stay on the medication was a difficult question though he was not keen to stop.

For panic disorder, there is a genetic component predisposing people to the attacks. Isolated panic attacks are very common with up to 30 per cent of the population having one in a year. There are theories of chemicals and processes in the brain stem which become unbalanced or hypersensitive. For about half of panic sufferers, hyperventilation is a factor and this can be treated directly with breathing techniques. Treatment with drugs is quite effective, as is treatment of CBT, and those together initially may be best for

73

someone too anxious and sleep deprived to cope. But if you take drugs to cope with anxiety you risk learning that this is the way to cope and then do not learn other strategies. The doctor must be careful in how he prescribes drugs. What message does he give? If it is "You need drugs and you are not able to help yourself in any other way" this is an excellent recipe for long-term dependence. Or is it "These will help for a short time so you can move on to other methods, to improve your thinking and make yourself stronger"? The second does sound better.

Just to complicate things we have a marvellous placebo effect. A powerful doctor gives you a magic pill and you naturally feel better. Even when the pill is a placebo or dummy pill there are positive effects. In fact for some conditions, including panic, effective medicine is only just better than placebo on average. This seems like a cognitive effect, learning there is a cure and being optimistic. Placebos even have side effects which is harder to explain. If it is a cognitive effect it may well be mediated by the body producing its own internal medicine. The power of intention and attention is strong even when the medium is medication rather than a psychological therapy. General anxiety and panic disorder are susceptible to a good placebo response. OCD is less easily fooled.

We also feel better at certain times of day, in good weather or after different types of food. These are all normal parts of our physical environment which change. But their effect on our nervous system, while obvious subjectively, is again too subtle to be easily comprehended by biochemical science. There are practical problems in studying these areas which are discussed later.

Internal communication

In past times the main health problems in the world could be seen to have external causes. Infections are caused by viruses, bacteria and micro-organisms which are external. Not having enough food or vitamins are again external problems. But these have now been overtaken by problems of internal balance and control. Heart disease and cancer have external factors, such as smoking, but are largely a breakdown of internal communication and balance. This is reflected in the medical therapies which aim themselves at the communication, balance, and immune system mechanisms.

As the nervous system is the most complex part of the body, it is no surprise that mental illnesses from a physical perspective relate to breakdowns in the internal functioning of the brain. Genetic factors predispose to anxiety and external factors push the brain out of balance. This imbalance then persists. The dysfunction in the nervous system in turn affects other systems such as the immune system. Anxiety reduces your life expectancy and greatly worsens the risks for cardio-vascular disease. Anxiety and depression are becoming major disabilities in world health.

Mind body relationships

In the life sciences a major mystery is how the two sides of life are related. How is subjective intelligence, which we all experience, connected to the objective intelligence we can see in the physical body? Both aspects are intelligent and they clearly are connected somehow. A physical blow on my head affects my conscious experience. I become unconscious. If I exercise my subjective free will and decide to do something exhilarating like a parachuting, my physiology will definitely be affected with my brain chemistry and cardiovascular system also jumping.

There is some knowledge of the parallels and correspondence between the subjective and objective worlds. Subjective anxiety is associated with an increased pulse, breathing and skin conductance, and hormonal changes in the blood. Changes in the brain are also recognized, though this has been hard to study at a chemical level. You cannot take samples directly from the brain easily in people and the poor old laboratory animals do not easily tell us their subjective experience. Ethics are also rightly problematic. Anxiety may be presumed in animals that are threatened or abused but this work is not a pleasant occupation. More subtle feelings may not be experienced by animals and if they are they cannot tell us.

Recent advances in brain scanning have allowed us to see which parts of the brain are active in different subjective states and during different tasks. This is starting to turn the table on the biologist. In the past it was assumed that the physical biology had primacy and subjective mental states had to follow. This is true at a very gross level. If a part of my brain associated with receiving vision from the left side of the world is grossly damaged or destroyed by injury or a stroke, then I can no longer experience sight from this side. But the question arises as to how much can the brain change and how can change be affected. I cannot regrow a large area of the brain lost to a stroke. It used to be assumed the brain had little or no ability to change and regrow in adult life. But now the brain is seen to have much more potential and more plasticity. Neurones do grow and new connections are made. We already know that suffering stress reduces this plasticity and potential growth. We are starting to see that psychological intervention can lead to changes in brain functioning. The mind can lead the brain.

The drug industry has the positive motive drive to produce drugs that alleviate suffering and cure illness. There is also a bad drive to increase the demand for drugs and so to increase profits. The second drive prefers drugs which alleviate suffering but do not cure. Lifelong dependence or reliance on a drug is more profitable. In many areas of medicine, like hypertension, peptic ulcer, or mental illness, we have produced drugs that alleviate symptoms or retard the illness process but do not cure. They do not lead to a future life free from drugs. This is not only caused by the bad driver in the pharmaceutical industry. The knowledge available at chemical level is not complete enough for us to find cures easily for most illnesses from simple drugs.

There is an ironic parallel here with Psychoanalysis. The good analyst wants to cure the patient or support their complete recovery. The dark side of the Force wants the client to remain in treatment indefinitely as this is easier, less stressful and more profitable. Sadly this frequently occurs. There is the same problem of incomplete knowledge. Both in pharmacology and analysis there is some accurate

From Anxiety To Peace

knowledge. But both schools of knowledge are incomplete and both need knowledge from another level.

Deeper levels of the physiology are more potent

The knowledge and intelligence at deeper layers underlie the functioning of the more visible superficial levels. DNA can be said to be a basic level of the body as it contains the knowledge in seed form that grows the body in the first place. It can grow replacement cells and continuously guides production of new proteins and enzymes to maintain the body's structure and metabolism. Currently the focus is on all the individual genes and their sequence chromosomes and how these relate to the body's characteristics and susceptibility to disease. We are not yet much interested in what the level below DNA is, but we should be. The study of individual subatomic particles in physics was fascinating and led to Nobel prizes being won, but it is a Unified Field theory underlying all the particles that answers the big questions of how the universe works.

The internal pharmacy

Because our minds and senses are clouded, or not fully developed, we tend to see our bodies objectively rather than feel them subjectively. We ourselves create an apparent split between mind and body. Because of this split we have forgotten our own abilities to keep in balance. Our ability to eat correctly, to keep fit, and to heal ourselves when imbalance occurs seem hidden. We know that the drugs used in psychiatry are hitting natural receptor sites. Opiates interact with receptors for natural opiates such as endorphins. We produce our own endorphins internally and can vary these through changes of mental state and activity. Obsessional jogging is a well-known example. Antidepressants hit the receptors for natural amines. Cannabis has its own natural analogues including chemicals that affect mood and memory mechanisms.

The great advantage of natural internal chemicals is their being perfectly designed for us and being in the right part of the brain to do their job. Therefore they are much less likely to be toxic or cause side-effects. There should be much more emphasis on the most obvious natural supporters of physical health. These are diet, sleep and exercise. There is great interest in diet and exercise to address the obesity epidemic but the effects on mental health are also very positive. Exercise is surprisingly effective in elevating mood and self-esteem. Sleep is starting to be recognised as important but struggles to overcome our established culture of late-night pizza and TV.

Another major mystery in psychiatry is why, when, and how episodes of mental illness end. Even severe illnesses usually have spontaneous remission. Panic disorder and OCD are the most episodic of the anxiety states and tend to be worse for bouts of a few months. But how the brain comes back into balance is unknown. Drugs may reduce symptoms, which is much appreciated, as when you are suffering serious mental illness every day improved can be a huge saving of pain. But drugs do not stop the episode and this is one reason for continuing them even when you feel much better. The episode may still be in process just masked by the drugs. The other reason is to prevent future episodes starting.

As we still do not understand the biology of normal mood sufficiently well we cannot study spontaneous remission or natural cures easily. The placebo effect may well use natural endogenous drugs but our ability to study this is limited.

Rest is a marvellous therapy for illness and for the stresses of life. In addition to good sleep we can benefit from regular practice of a stress management or relaxation technique.

The analytic nature of biological science needs to mature to understand better the abstract levels of intelligence and more unified modes of functioning. It turns out to be hard to interfere with the body using single drugs without incurring side-effects. In the environment it is similarly hard to interfere with individual chemicals or species of life without causing problems somewhere else in the ecosystem. Very complex systems defy superficial intellectual analysis. We need to use deeper and unifying levels of intelligence.

We naturally experience health as more than the absence of disease. Positive health is a feeling of physical energy and fitness and of normal functions working well. Likewise mental health includes happiness, enjoying rest and enjoying dynamic activity. If we feel

78

deviation from this it is obvious to us. We have a supremely sensitive internal technology to feel imbalance. But we do not go within ourselves to use the internal pharmacy to naturally rebalance our functioning. When we use modern medicine we have to wait till imbalance is quite advanced before a specific illness and treatment can be selected.

Knower, Knowing and Known in Biological Medicine

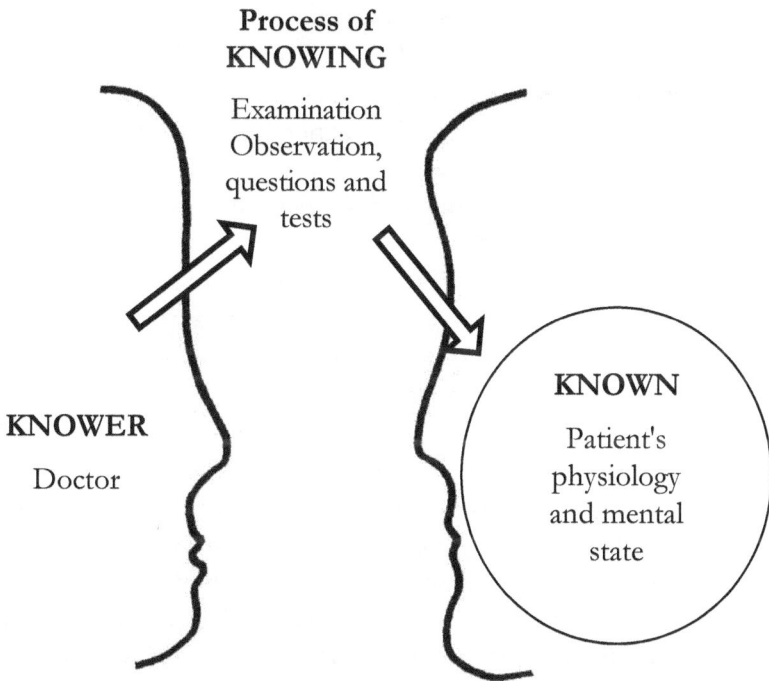

**Process of
KNOWING**

Examination
Observation,
questions and
tests

KNOWER

Doctor

KNOWN

Patient's
physiology
and mental
state

The doctor as Knower, owning the knowledge and the language

For the doctor-patient relationship, biological medicine has the classic Knower to Known set up. The doctor is definitely the Knower and the patient the object to be studied. The process value is the doctor's examination, interrogation and tests. At the extreme this is jokingly called veterinary psychiatry when a patient might as well be an animal as his opinion is not sought and he does not need to know anything.

One reason for this Knower to Known pattern is that the knowledge and the very language of science are obscure and difficult. Even doctors have difficulty understanding the language in a different speciality to their own. Doctors struggle to comprehend the basic sciences which underlie the scientific understanding of biological science. And they do not expect their patients to understand the technical scientific details. In fact if a patient said to me that his state of mind was due to dysregulation of his dopamine receptors I would wonder if this was evidence of delusional thinking, even if I myself was thinking about this mechanism. We do not expect patients to link their subjective experience to such an objective molecular
explanation. Only the biological doctors think they have the flexibility in their minds to do that.

A major reason why this language is so hard to access is that it does not link easily to everyday life or subjective feelings. The theory of anxiety based on noradrenaline and brain-stem centres only links directly to the taking of amine-related drugs and avoiding legal or illegal stimulant drugs. This is not surprising since drugs were the basis of the theory. But it does not relate much to food or daily routines, or weather, or other aspects even of biological life.

This isolated type of knowledge, which makes sense only to the doctor, tends to leave patients more dependent and powerless. There has been some progress recently in patient education and widening our biological approaches. The Internet has accelerated people's access to drug information. Knowledge of at least the effects and side-effects of drugs are no longer the doctor's private possession. These arguments are not intended to undermine the doctor's position as a holder of specialist knowledge. It is very useful to have highly trained specialists with experience and understanding. But unless the magic bullet is completely effective specialists have to do more teaching. Only wizards are allowed to keep their wisdom secret.

There has also been recognition that general physical health is very important in mental illness. Previously it was presumed that

80

poor diet, daily routine, lack of exercise, smoking etc. were caused by the weakness of mind. There was less awareness that all these could be worsening mental illness, as well as causing the usual physical health problems. Most major mental illnesses greatly reduce life expectation and this is mainly due to increased physical illness not death through suicide.

Physical health is now seen as much more important in the approach to mental illness. Best practice for management of any severe mental illness would emphasise keeping a regular sleep pattern. Exercise has become more popular in the treatment of depression. Diet is important if only because many drugs encourage weight gain.

Caroline and the Biological Psychiatrist

When Caroline visits this psychiatrist he is full of questions about her physical health and does a physical exam to look for heart disease, maybe mitral valve prolapse, thyroid imbalance, or hyperventilation which throws the blood chemistry out. He does blood tests and an electrocardiogram. He is very attentive to her use of drugs including caffeine which stimulates panic, alcohol which causes panic on the rebound, cannabis which can surprisingly trigger off episodes of panic disorder, and the more exotic drugs. He focuses on the exact symptoms of panic, their rapid onset, and duration. He also asks about depression which is a common partner to panic.

Panic attacks are defined by the symptoms and there is less interest in underlying causes. In practice the biological psychiatrist will know about the cognitive behavioral approach and consider this as a therapeutic option. But he may see some people as having pure panic disorder apparently unrelated to situations or triggers. Their fear is of panic itself. The biological or drug approaches are likely to be more favoured when there are no obvious phobic associations or anxiety levels are so high the patient finds concentration and co-operation with psychological therapy difficult. The presence of depression will also make drug treatment more likely.

This assessment finds that Caroline does have the right symptoms for panic and in addition has depressive symptoms. Agoraphobia he considers to be moderate and driven by the panic attacks. He advises her to stop all caffeine, over a couple of weeks to avoid withdrawal, and avoid alcohol. He prescribes an antidepressant which despite the name is also effective in reducing panic. He did not discover many symptoms of hyperventilation otherwise he would have considered breathing exercises.

Perhaps unwittingly he makes an important cognitive intervention. He reassures her she does not have a life-threatening illness and strongly suggests that treatment will work. This will be good cognitive therapy if he succeeds in replacing Caroline's catastrophic interpretation with his own more optimistic ideas.

A few weeks go by and the treatment has started working. Caroline has only occasional and very minor attacks and her mood is much better. Will she spontaneously stop all her avoidance behavior? She may do but she may also need some behavioral prompting to regain her confidence. An interesting decision arises as to when to stop her medication. There we find out how biological the doctor is. Does he tell her she has a genetic and physiological weakness leaving her prone to panic disorder and suggested she take medication for a long time? He could temporise by advising a course of 6 to 12 months and stopping, but then consider a much longer time if she relapses at that point. Or does he advise more cognitive behavioral strategies to now strengthen her-self in the future? Ideally he would share different options with her. In the short term the biological explanation can be reassuring. But in the long term it can undermine other possibilities. If you believe you have a lifelong physical deficiency it is harder to look beyond physical treatment. If the doctor does not share knowledge and simply tells Caroline that she will be ill if she does not take medication this becomes even harder.

Education and sharing decisions do loosen up the doctor-patient relationship. The patient is allowed to be a bit of a Knower. To change the pattern more fundamentally we need to re-examine the mind-body split. Biological science gets the patient to report their feelings to the doctor so he can make a diagnosis and assess progress.

82

It does not use the patient's observation of their own body more directly. The subjective experience of the patient is given over to the doctor to translate into objective knowledge which may then be fed back to the patient. As we have seen, this knowledge may not be in a language that is very meaningful to the patient. Our senses form the natural link between our subjective experience and physical body. If we accept a helpless and dependent position, this link is one way only.

The mind can sense how out of shape of the body is. Biologists do not use the mind to control the body. Even the use of the senses is not encouraged. Too much interest in how your body feels is easily labelled neurotic or hypochondriacal. Women are often accused of this and they do consult doctors more with minor symptoms. It is interesting that women live longer than men. Are they more sensitive to small imbalances? Tough men ignore minor illnesses but maybe suffer the consequences.

Doing no harm

One of the lessons doctors learn is to do no harm. This is especially important in biological medicine. Drugs represent powerful but often incomplete knowledge. In prescribing them we must avoid side-effects, damage and addiction which can be worse than the original illness. Benzodiazepines can cause sedation in the day, muscle weakness, falls and memory loss. We must be careful not to undermine the patient's own strengths and abilities by persuading them that they are helpless victims of a disturbed physiology.

The same logic applies to the non-prescribed drugs that people take themselves. The damage of alcohol and illegal drugs far outweighs their benefits. We know this, but both patients and doctors often prefer to forget. We tend to neglect our own addictions and turn a blind eye to those in our patients. If a patient with insomnia is taking too much caffeine, it is ludicrous to give sleeping tablets. If someone has depression and panic fuelled by alcohol why prescribe another drug? Stopping harmful drugs is good advice if you are ill and even better if you are not.

83

If you are consuming small amounts of alcohol, cannabis, caffeine, nicotine, analgesics or antacids, and are unable to stop this, you have a good signal that you are under stress and not coping so well. A healthy physiology does not need these props. To achieve and maintain perfect health we develop our own balancing and homeostatic mechanisms. We do not build a strong structure by using external supports.

The best place for drugs is in the more severe anxiety where your psychology may be overwhelmed. You may become unable to use your own mind easily to recover equilibrium. But even here, the drugs should be used to support psychological, behavioral, and social changes where possible. It is important to be optimistic about recovery, to a life beyond medication. Accepting a life sentence on medication should be a last resort.

Connections to the Diversity of Life

Biological medicine has a dominant place in the diversity of therapies if we use money spent as a measure. It has not related much to other therapies because politically it has not had to. The tide is beginning to turn and patients now expect options of non-drug therapies or for more serious illness, drugs plus other approaches. Scientifically we are beginning to understand the mental parallels of changes in neurotransmitters.

In Society we have a culture of expecting pills for treatment and a strong culture of recreational drug use. In the physical environment there is increasing recognition of the role of biorhythms linking the physiology to the outer cycles of time. From research on meditation we see different states of mind have their own physiological states.

Despite the strong science in biological medicine it has stalled at a level of fascinating molecular differences. It should know there is a whole new pool of knowledge in quantum physics and beyond, but currently it is reluctant to take the plunge.

Medicine's preoccupation with illness means we have more scientific knowledge about illnesses than about health and very little about higher states of consciousness. Every state of consciousness has a corresponding style of functioning in the physiology. Enlightenment would correspond to an ideal state of physical health. Just as psychoanalysis was preoccupied with sick states of mind, biological medicine has been over concerned with imbalance and physical illness. This has made it a poorer method for understanding health and the holistic functioning of life. In the future there will be more study of health and higher states of consciousness.

Evidence for Drug Therapy in Anxiety

Here we look at drug therapy alone. Other biological approaches such as breathing techniques are examined later. Drugs are used mainly in Panic Disorder, Agoraphobia, and OCD when these are more severe or complicated by depression. Many anti-depressants are active against panic attacks. Benzodiazepines have a place in severe states but usually only short term Response rates are good but CBT would normally be used as well for longer-term progress. Drugs are rarely used in Specific Phobias. Use in Social Phobia is more controversial and psychological methods preferred by most. If there are particular debilitating physical symptoms such as tremor or palpitations then Beta-blocker drugs can be very useful. Blocking these bodily symptoms can stop the vicious circle of physical symptoms increasing mental anxiety which then increases physical symptoms.

Generalised Anxiety responds short-term to benzodiazepines but these have a high risk of dependency and tolerance developing. Some anti-depressants such as the Serotonin Specific Re-uptake Inhibitors (SSRIs) have some effect on anxiety for about two thirds of people. People prone to anxiety and depression may have a short form of the gene for serotonin transfer in neurones. Paroxetine is the most studied SSRI. Tolerance is much less likely to develop but psychological dependence is a risk. Buspirone is a different type of drug that is used in GAD. This supports a theory that there may be an excess of 5HT in some pathways in GAD. For anxiety traits methods other than medication will be needed.

OCD is treated with a combination of BT, CT, and medication if severe. Anti-depressants which increase 5HT activity, including an

85

older one Clomipramine, can be very effective. In the most severe cases anti-psychotic drugs can be helpful.

Which people are comfortable with Drug Therapy?

Medication suits people who do not want to do the work involved in psychological therapies. This may reflect not wanting to be the Knower. If anxiety is a longer term problem you may need to challenge this avoidance of taking more control.

Medicine is not so appropriate for people with addictive tendencies though they will be tempted to choose this. Nor is it sensible to start new drugs for anxiety if you are currently taking drugs that worsen anxiety such as alcohol, caffeine and cannabis.

Medicines are obviously less appealing if you fear side-effects, though trialling different medicines should minimise this problem.

Qualities of the mind identified in Biological Psychiatry

∞ Levels of biological intelligence underlie the physical body
∞ Every state of mind has a corresponding state of physiology
∞ Mental imbalance reflects imbalance in the nervous system
∞ Rest counteracts imbalance and stress

∞ Chapter 6 ∞
Group Therapy –
More than the Sum of the Parts

Every individual is defined by the groups they belong to: Irish, living in Birmingham, Catholic, football fan, school teacher, female, 30 something age group, Green Peace member, Sagittarius, cat lover, family member. We gain support, safety and enjoyment from our groups because we are social animals. We can also find new groups a source of anxiety.

In many cultures there has been a loss of crucial natural groups such as large families. Fragmentation of society has led to previously important institutions such as churches being less prominent. At the same time group therapy has become more popular. Group therapy can be more powerful than individual treatment. It can be effective, it may be cheaper and it can be fun.

Groups can use almost any paradigm or school of therapy. In addition they have their own special effects through the group process and interaction. Groups generate strong feelings and are threatening if not well run. Groups are particularly suited to self-help approaches as they dilute or avoid the dependency on the therapist as the Knower.

Anxiety is a great focus for group therapy. This allows members to learn and gain strength from others' experiences. Social confidence can be built in a safe setting. Therapy is less intense with regard to the individual doctor-patient relationship but patient to patient relationships become important.

Therapeutic groups have rules to ensure safety, respect, and trust for their members. To increase safety and trust, groups may be exclusive, that is closed to new members, with strong expectations about confidentiality and of members turning up reliably. Confidentiality may be underlined by members not being allowed to have contact with each other outside the group. However for other groups

87

there may be a positive expectation that social relationships will develop between members or that the group itself will become a long-term social network.

The group needs to be clear what its goal is and so what work it will be doing. This varies between types of therapy. In relaxation or assertiveness training the work is extremely focused and the goal is clear, that is to learn particular skills, and there is avoidance of the group being side-tracked into emotional catharsis. Groups tend to achieve more when trust and safety are well established and the group becomes cohesive. This allows more sharing and honest communication, generating a strong group identity or group consciousness. It gives a strong sense that members are not alone in their suffering and validates them as individuals. In this context the group can serve to instil hope or to give permission for change. It enables feedback to be given which is often lacking in an individualistic society. The intensity of feedback needs to be tolerable as the power of the group also has potential to overwhelm an anxious member. The stronger the external boundaries of the group, the more special the environment within the group becomes. This allows the boundaries between people within the group to be relaxed because they are protected by the wider boundary around the whole group. Greater sharing, support and sensitivity develop within the group. This closeness and belonging in itself can be a positive and very reassuring experience.

Self-help groups may be organised around a particular problem such as panic or Agoraphobia. They have the advantage of being able to combine many different approaches. These include didactic sessions run by individual members and sharing of strategies found to be helpful. The group can also use looser more creative approaches and being composed of peers may seem less judgemental. Other people such as partners or carers may be involved and the group may overlap with social support networks. Some groups interface with professional support systems or even graduate to become professional organisations. The freedom of the self-help group allows it to integrate ideas from different paradigms looking at anxiety from different perspectives. The sense of common purpose in a group

88

generates hope and a strong ethos of recovery and progress. Social and emotional support combines with knowledge-based assistance. Successful graduates who have overcome their fears inspire people whose journey is just starting.

Greg was a 30 year old business man who had coped with a degree of Agoraphobia and panic during his twenties. As he became more successful in business the stress of long days, business worries and an increased demand for travel resulted in his anxiety state worsening and interfering with his business.

Being a pragmatic man he took medication which stopped the worse panic attacks. He also did a course of CBT which helped him relax and travel a bit more. He remained very fearful of longer distance travel and flying. He was making progress but decided to join a self-help group to do everything he could to improve. The group showed him that people use many different strategies and they encouraged him to think more creatively. As he was wealthy, some-one jokingly suggested he learn to fly. He realized this would teach him much more about flying, give him a sense of mastery, and might be fun instead of terrifying. So he did this and finally conquered his fears.

The Family

Family therapy uses a special group because it is one that continues in real life with the exception of the therapist. Here the members of the group comprise important parts of each other's natural environment as parents, children, or partners. High energy relationships already exist and for this reason therapy can sometimes be very fast. Again many approaches are possible in a family setting. At the simplest level families are involved in education around the anxiety disorder being suffered by one member. Family can become co-therapists in a Behavior Therapy program such as helping the person with Agoraphobia to go out more. However the special forms of family therapy use the systems of the family itself in the therapeutic method. These recognize and use unique family structures and processes. For example, a time of crisis is seen positively as a time of opportunity for potential change in a family which has got stuck. Symptoms which seem obviously negative have a positive role in a homoeostatic mechanism. The child is too anxious to go to school but his behavior is serving to make parents work together and spend time together in a relationship at risk of separation. Systems of family therapy recognize the family as having a definite structure and functioning. The family has its own consciousness with memories, self-interaction, balance mechanisms and creativity.

Causation is usually complicated and sometimes circular. The mother is anxious because the father is alcoholic; he drinks because of his teenage daughter's misbehavior; she acts out because of her mother's Agoraphobia. Symptoms in an individual can be seen as a problem for the whole family. This wider view can be very powerful. Treating the depressed mother as an individual may never be success-ful if the father and daughter are left out.

Marriage is a unique relationship and a concentration of family life. Two individuals come together to form a greater wholeness. Love is the common experience that gives at least the flavour of the transcendental unity between two people. Within this the creativity of differences can play. The difficulty of finding and maintaining this reality today is very evident in music and drama where searching for love and falling in love are so dominant. Less easily found are examples and role models of mature marriages beyond the honey-moon.

Families have their problems but they also have tremendous strengths and resources. We can make use of the family members who are healthy and of the extended family. We may learn from past generations. The larger family consciousness can support and help repair a local weakness.

Group consciousness and the power of a group

Group therapy, including family therapy, has many positive aspects. The group has more power and change can be more rapid. Anxious symptoms can be acknowledged to have positive values and crises are also opportunities. Group therapy naturally has a positive view of other people as being potentially helpful. There is an expectation of taking

From Anxiety To Peace

responsibility for others but also of being responsible for your-self individually and as a whole group.

The successful group generates a collective consciousness with its own intelligence and dynamism. An individual within the group can experience this wider consciousness. An individual can speak for the whole group. What they feel may be the feeling of the group, of the collective consciousness. In more ancient cultures individuals have been acknowledged as speaking for the feelings of a whole society, sometimes through dreams. This is less obvious in individual-istic societies and an experience of this in group therapy can be very striking.

In a successful group we see that the desire for individual self-sufficiency is not incompatible with group unity. In fact they are complimentary. Unity is crucial to the group's success and this wholeness of the group is made up of the diverse individuals coming together. The unity of the group supports this diversity and diversity in turn structures the greater unity. Just as the many and different cells make up an individual body, mainly individual people make up collective consciousness.

Another complimentary relationship is between boundaries and unboundedness. It is tempting to cut down boundaries in order to increase communication and intimacy within a group. Outside of the therapy situation this may be culturally sanctioned on a temporary basis in certain situations such as parties or festival days. As Madonna sings "I want to lose control, I want to free my soul." But rules have a purpose, to protect individuals and channel our unboundedness safely. Without rules the many instruments of the orchestra could not make music together. A group that is too disinhibited and not well supervised is unsafe.

Caroline in Group Therapy

Caroline tries a self-help group for panic sufferers. She finds this a much more normal setting closer to some social groups she belongs to. She is happy to be welcomed by fellow panickers and glad to find they seem to be pretty normal people.

91

Indeed most of them are very pleasant perhaps because anxious people tend to avoid conflict. They have many different views on panic and between them have visited therapists from most parts of the Unified Field Chart. Caroline can listen to ideas and advice without having to immediately respond. She has more sense of choice. She does try a breathing exercise someone found useful and she arranges to go on some trips with a couple of other women to support each other's confidence.

The group is neither very high energy nor regimented but there is a strong sense of mutual care. People care about any members not doing so well. The relationships lack the brilliant intensity of psychoanalysis but have the value of simple genuineness and equality. Caroline finds that her interest and advice to others is appreciated and this increases her own sense of empowerment.

When Caroline has recovered she leaves the group as she wants to move on in her life and she does have other supports among her family and friends. She does keep in contact with one group member who became a friend. She remains an important person in her life who has shared a valuable experience.

Prior to joining her group, Caroline had become withdrawn and passive tending towards helplessness. The sense of purpose and liveliness of the group had a direct effect on her becoming more active and positive. She was inspired by the progress of others.

Playing with multiple relationships

In terms of Knower, Knowing and Known relationships there are many possibilities in groups. The group therapist can observe the group, enter into its processes, or be observed. A second therapist can take up a different position and commonly one therapist relates to the whole group and one to individuals. Two therapists can also interact with each other, for example to model how different opinions can be expressed and resolved. Then there are all the patient to patient interactions and the patient to whole group interactions. The patient may get feedback from the therapist or from another group member or from the whole group, which will be the most powerful. Understanding how you as an individual affect other people in the group is an excellent way to learn how you affect other people in your life generally.

Knower, Knowing and Known in Group Therapy

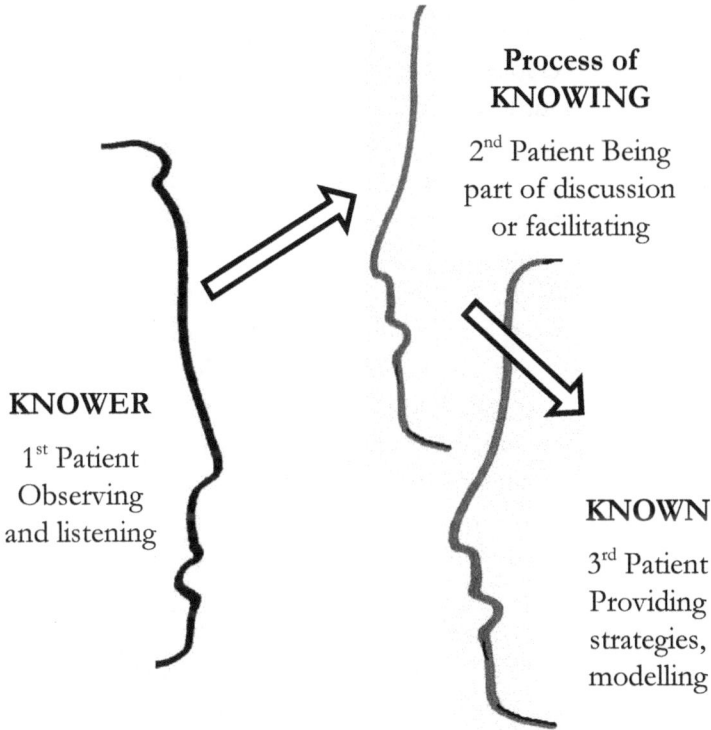

Process of KNOWING

2nd Patient Being part of discussion or facilitating

KNOWER

1st Patient Observing and listening

KNOWN

3rd Patient Providing strategies, modelling

Therapists may use strategies in a group which overtly play with the Knower, Knowing and Known positions. People may deliberately swap chairs to symbolise the swapping of positions. Role-play can be used, or talking to an empty chair to represent somebody not present. Psychodrama is a whole school of therapy where dramas may be acted out representing parts of the person's life or personality.

Multiple patterns are possible. In a self-help group different members can take up the three positions. For example one can be listening and observing (Knower) to another who is explaining how they cope with anxiety (Known) while another mediates or asks questions (Process of Knowing). Overall the patients in the group create the process of knowing and this is the dominant position.

Connections to the Diversity of Life

Group processes can be found all over the Society column of the Unified Field Chart. Because the social sciences are not well organised, neither are group therapies. Groups can link across from the individual therapies to the various levels of society. Group principles can be found useful in a schools and the work-place. BT, CT and Psychoanalysis can be all be applied to a couple or a family or a group. Groups are often used to teach relaxation for the body and to support exposure therapy in the physical environment.

The essence of group therapy is found in the dynamics of a group creating a greater whole. This is the key connecting principle going up the Society section. This is not yet understood in the detail or mathematics that we can find in the physical sciences. Science still needs to develop the subjective side of the Chart. TM research has contributed to the understanding of group conscious through coherence effects. Group meditation is deeper than individual practice. Both the individual and the group have their basis in consciousness.

From group theory we appreciate that it is possible to learn from and to enjoy other people. We do not need to be shy in therapy. Individuals contribute to group consciousness and are supported by the group. Groups need to balance boundaries and unboundedness. Unboundedness is the nature of life at its deepest level but life expresses itself and grows through boundaries. Respect for other people, social rules and morality are necessary to channel our unbounded nature in relationships.

The group has its own reality beyond the individual. The power of group dynamics and the group's wider strength can allow trans-formation in the individual to occur. These point to the larger Self or being of the group. It encourages us to look to new goals both in the

94

transformation of families and society and also towards higher states of consciousness.

Effectiveness of Group Therapy in Anxiety

Group therapy is used successfully with a behavioral or CBT approach for most types of anxiety. Where symptoms are severe you are more likely to need individual help. Medication is always prescribed in an individual therapy but this can be parallel to a group therapy using CBT. Groups provide more scope for practice of skills and getting feedback in a safe place. For Panic Disorder and Agoraphobia, groups are useful but it is best to have a good individual assessment first to see which factors are important for you.

Specific Phobias such as flying do very well with group therapy as there is such a clear common goal. For GAD and OCD group therapy can teach skills in the short term. When these disorders are chronic and hard to resolve groups provide longer-term support. You can learn how to cope with problems and improve quality of life even when these are not being cured.

Family therapy is well evidenced for the treatment of childhood anxiety and is not used enough where the identified sufferer is an adult. Again this can be used as a supplement to CBT.

Which people are comfortable with Group Therapy?

Groups may be too threatening for extremely shy people. If the group is very focussed and has a clear curriculum, as in a CBT group, the social demands are much less and you may benefit from the limited social interaction.

For less structured groups you need to be able to accept some feed-back. A paranoid attitude would be less than ideal. Groups best suit people who are flexible in their Knower, Knowing and Known positions. That means you can listen as well as talk.

Groups are great if you are feeling all alone in your problem and would like others' support.

Qualities of the mind identified in Group Therapy

∞ The collective mind is more than the sum of the individuals
∞ Individual and collective consciousness affect each other
∞ Strong collective consciousness supports transformation in individual experience

∞ Chapter 7 ∞
Natural Medicine – A Diversity of Therapies

Natural medicine is a growing fast. Americans spend as much on this as on modern primary care medicine. Every magazine tells you about aromatherapy or some frightening cleansing regime. The public are making a protest vote against scientific medicine. This vote could have been more wisely cast. Much of what is sold today in the name of natural medicine has very little tradition behind it and even less evidence of effectiveness. This has enabled the mainstream medical establishment to dismiss it all as unworthy.

What is it that people are protesting about? They want to know how to stay healthy, to stay free from anxiety. They want to address underlying causes of illness. They want medicine without side-effects. They want a language that is closer to their own experience of life. Natural therapies can be organised according to the five senses, time, and energy or life-force. This leads to a more familiar language.

Some techniques can be aimed at treating anxiety while others are more preventative and look at creating a healthy life-style to remain calm. Most traditional systems recognise a basic element in the constitution that predisposes to anxiety if out of balance. This element tends to predominate in nervous people.

Hearing

Hearing is the most subtle of the five senses and it is often used in meditation through the use of sounds, music or mantras. This will be considered in the next chapter. Music is also commonly used for relaxation. Different beats or rhythms have different effects as we all experience. If you are stuck in a habit of listening to very loud and fast music you might want to try expanding your play list.

The overall level of sound is high for many our lives. A main change in the environment over the last 300 years has been the

97

increase in ambient noise in cities. Why is the country-side so relaxing? Because it is so quiet. Natural sounds such as birds and running water also have more harmony with our physiology. Reducing noise in your life can reduce stress even if the methods are technological like double glazing.

Touch

Touch is a very intimate sense. Contact between mother and child is supportive of the baby's development. Touch is in short supply in some cultures and the fear of child abuse is in danger of making society touch phobic. Touching, holding and caressing someone is a natural response to soothe them if they are anxious or upset.

Massage is a more prolonged expression of touch. Massage has many types from specific musculo-skeletal, through general relaxation, to mind-body connections. Some systems see the body as connecting to the mind or life-force through special points in the body. Massage is one technique to encourage or balance flows of energy. Acupuncture points may be massaged as well as needled (which is a more acute sort of touch). Ayur Veda uses Marma points but this speciality is less well preserved. Doing daily Abhyanga, or oil massage, yourself is part of an Ayur Vedic daily routine and is particularly good for anxiety. Sesame or coconut oil are commonly used. Specific massages for the head are also prescribed. These are extremely calming and without the side-effects of medication, but with the side effect of having oily hair.

Using touch through massage is a very different approach to anxiety from a talking therapy. Not all cultures are so predisposed to talk about their feelings and fears. One group of people who can especially benefit from massage are those who have been badly traumatised or tortured. Talking about their experience may be too hard, at least until a very trusting safe relationship has been established. Massage is a more acceptable form of help and can address the tension that is stored in the body after extreme stress.

98

Sight

The optic nerves are the widest highway on which information enters the brain. The quality of what we see has a great influence on our state of mind and level of anxiety. Television has the ability to push many stressful images very quickly and with rapid changes of image into our nervous system. This can increase stress levels particularly late in the evening when we should be preparing to sleep. Of course pleasant sights have a positive effect. Colours are used in therapy and are used in our environments. We all think carefully before painting our rooms.

Light is used as a distinct therapy and is supplemented by the use of gems. Gems are interesting as they are universally seen as precious because they look so beautiful. People also desire to wear them. This is to complement their own beauty but gems are also said to have effects on the physiology. Some systems of natural medicine see the body as having finer levels of intelligence including a level of light. Gems interact with and strengthen this level. Modern science definitely sees the body as having finer levels right down through sub-atomic particles to the quantum fields but it does not see these finest levels as being much use for therapy yet.

Light therapy has a specific use in the treatment of depression because the circadian rhythm is disturbed in depression, especially when depression is seasonal in nature. Light therapy helps reset the natural cycle in depression but unfortunately it does not work so well in the much commoner rhythm disturbance that is insomnia.

Taste

Diet is a modern obsession and ironically so since so many countries now do have enough to eat. Somehow the Western diet has gone out of control with obesity the major health risk of our time. Food processing and additives have disguised food so that we like what is bad for us. This is compounded by our neglecting our natural ability to judge food through our senses. Using the intellect to analyse the chemical make-up of food can of course be useful but this has displaced our sensory skills which have evolved over millennia to guide us to healthy eating.

99

Food is often used to soothe ourselves when stressed or anxious. In Ayurvedic terms this usually means foods that are sweet, sour, salty and hot. No surprise that this describes many fast foods which we use to combat the stress caused by our lives being too fast in the first place.

We also ingest foods and drinks which have more powerful effects on anxiety. Caffeine is the prime suspect. This greatly increases the risk of anxiety and panic in particular. Alcohol reduces anxiety short term and so is used to self-medicate for social anxiety. However the rebound increases anxiety. If you are particularly nervous in the morning or panic in the early hours you should definitely look at your alcohol intake. Cannabis is more variable with many experiencing some calming affect but cannabis can also precipitate very bad panic and depersonalisation, an unpleasant feeling of being detached from reality. Obviously your system will be clearer if you reduce and stop these drugs. Drinking more water is one simple way of living a cleaner life and it is perhaps no coincidence that with the decline in smoking cigarettes we see bottles of water being carried around everywhere.

On the positive side there are foods and drinks which have more concentrated positive effects. These are the herbs and spices known and valued throughout the world for their strong tastes and their medicinal effects. All food has specific effects on the constitution and the herbs simply have stronger effects. There are many traditions of herbal medicine. Some are just customary use of local herbs in cooking. Others have complex preparations of many herbs and minerals. Preparation may include enhancing the power of medicines through processes which are not clear to Western science such as dilution in homeopathy.

One common theme among traditions is that the structure of intelligence in nature is the same as that in our physiology. Herbal medicine tends to use the whole intelligence of the plant rather than an individual chemical. Again this is hard to fathom in Western bio-chemistry but the body is known to be very complex and using single chemicals as drugs has problems of side-effects due to this complexity.

100

Taste is part of the digestive system. The digestive tract takes in nourishment and also removes waste and impurities. The idea of detoxing and purifying the body has become very fashionable if only to balance periods of excessive nourishment. Again these practices are found in many systems and include fasting or eating lightly to allow the metabolism and digestion to focus on purification. Purging through vomiting or over-stimulating the bowels will be less appealing to many. Enemas are another option or colonic wash-outs for the brave. Ayur Veda uses a combined approach of Pancha Karma including light eating, herbs, oil massage, steam bath, and enemas. This is aimed at enhancing the elimination of toxins and waste through the tissues into the gut and out the other end. It is ideally done on a seasonal basis.

Smell

Our sense of smell is a more primitive sense and plugs straight in to our emotions. It supplements taste in our appreciation of food but has a wider effect on our appreciation of the environment. The smell of a building, a car, or a person, is important to us. As with taste, smells have specific effects on the physiology and some plants have strong special effects. These are the perfumes and essential oils. Aromatherapy is widely used on an informal basis and advice flows from every women's magazine. It appeals as being simple and non-invasive. We all desire to have nice smelling homes and we also experience that smells can be calming.

Natural Rhythms

Our body has many rhythms which are mirrored in the outside world. The most obvious is the 24 hour day and the seasonal changes. Women have a monthly cycle about the length of the moon's circuit. Less obvious but important are the shorter hormonal and metabolic cycles in the body with the main one being at 90 minutes. This is also the dream cycle time at night. Shorter still are the circulation time, about a minute, and the pulse, about a second. Breathing is usually about 4 times the heart rate at rest.

These rhythms help the body to stay in balance. In health the rhythms are stable and they are also in synchrony. Anxiety is often associated with disrupted and irregular rhythms. Sleep pattern is disturbed, menstruation irregular, digestion, both appetite and bowels, is variable. Unfortunately a vicious circle occurs with disturbed cycles such as sleep leading to more anxiety leading to even worse sleep.

Insomnia

Insomnia troubles over 60 million people in the USA and the costs run into many billions of dollars through direct costs of medical care and the indirect effects on job performance and absenteeism. Sometimes insomnia reflects another psychological or physical health problem, but most commonly it is a problem of rhythm and daily routine. Science has studied circadian rhythms and identified a least two clocks or 24-hour pacemakers in the hypothalamus. Some of the effects of light and dark are known as are mechanisms involving melatonin and amines (the same ones involved in mood). But this knowledge has not led to good cures for insomnia. Drugs provide short-term relief but long-term usually make things worse. From an Ayur Vedic perspective, insomnia is commonly due to disturbed Vata whose natural tendencies include being fast and variable. Imbalance leads to tiredness or anxiety in the day and variable or poor sleep. Caffeine is a great disrupter of sleep, especially for Vata types. As well as just keeping you awake, coffee also has the effect of weakening the 24 hour internal clock.

Ayur Veda distinguishes between types of insomnia according to the imbalance of the different Doshas. When Vata is the main problem then regularity of routine needs to be emphasised and established. Where Pitta is strong in the constitution, it is important not to go to bed too late. From about 10 p.m. to 2 a.m. Pitta becomes stronger. If you have strong Pitta tendencies and have not gone to bed early enough you may start to feel energised and hungry around this time and describe yourself as a night person, finding it hard to sleep till 1 or 2 a.m. as Pitta reduces. Kapha has characteristics of strength and stability and is less associated with rhythm disturbance. But a person with strong Kapha in their constitution needs to ensure they have long enough hours of sleep and not to disturb their sleep by eating too late in the evening because of the time needed to digest. Exercise will counteract the influence of Kapha and may best be taken during the Kapha time of day such as early evening.

Energy

There is some energy powering the body, some life-force. Science sees this is terms of chemical energy but natural traditions look at an energy which includes intelligence, connecting the body with its underlying intelligence or consciousness. This is also called Chi, Prana, Pneuma, and Vis Vitalis. There are many ways of enhancing or balancing energy including exercise, postures, breathing techniques and meditations.

The most superficial way to enhance your energy and feelings of energy being in balance is physical exercise. This has effects on the muscles, joints, and cardio-respiratory system to make you fitter. It can also combat anxiety by using up the adrenaline and energy generated by anxiety. In the extreme of panic the fight or flight response mobilises the body's resources for a burst of physical action. Unless you do actually run it is unlikely this energy is used as the body intended which pushes your energy out of balance. A chronicly stresses pituitary-adrenal axis makes you prone to further anxiety and to depression.

Some forms of exercise such as Yoga and Tai Chi use postures and sequences of movements. These improve flexibility and can be seen to improve blood flow. They also work by improving energy flow and mind-body coordination. Tai Chi is used for example in the elderly to improve balance. Other systems use manipulation or direction of attention to parts of the body. These include osteopathy, chiropractic and the Alexander technique. These may all have useful superficial mechanisms to improve posture, nerve positions, and spinal mechanics. Many schools additionally emphasise benefits on the level of energy flows to improve health more generally.

Breathing is basic to life and in some traditions there is a word for breath that also means life-force. In Western science we recognise hyperventilation as a big factor in anxiety and panic. Strangely when you hyperventilate you feel as if you are not breathing enough and so breathe more, making the situation worse. Over breathing causes the lungs to get rid of carbon dioxide too much and this affects your blood chemistry making it more alkaline. You then have symptoms of tingling, shakiness, light-headedness and feel very odd. Hyperventilation is caused partly by the over activation of the body, preparing it for physical action that never happens. It is also caused by incorrect breathing patterns. If you breath fast and shallow and by expanding the upper chest with your ribs, this tends to blow off carbon dioxide. If you breathe slowly and deeply by using your diaphragm to expand the bottom of the lungs, this counteracts hyperventilation. Simple breathing exercises encourage this type of breathing. If you have already blown off too much carbon dioxide you can reverse this by re-breathing, using a paper bag or cupped hands, to simply re-breathe some of it back in. Taking exercise makes the body use up oxygen and produces more carbon dioxide so this also combats the syndrome. This is why bag-pipe players keep on the march up and down.

Breathing is commonly used in relaxation or as a prelude to meditation. Breathing is a neutral activity to put attention on and can easily be settled by this attention. Again we can also see breathing as having subtle levels and feel life-giving energy in the breath.

Relaxation techniques may involve physical stretching or putting attention on the body, or breathing exercises. The senses can be used by listening to soothing sounds, looking at pleasant sights, using aromas, being touched in massage etc. There is a common relaxation response which can be easily invoked. The main ingredient is deciding to relax for a regular period each day. This response settles the heart rate and breathing and relaxes the muscles. These methods overlap with meditation. More mental meditation can be approached through the senses, for example from sight to inner visualisation. Breathing can also be felt as inner mental energy. More distinct

From Anxiety To Peace

meditations involve thinking techniques. These are discussed in the next chapter.

Knower, Knowing and Known in Natural Medicine

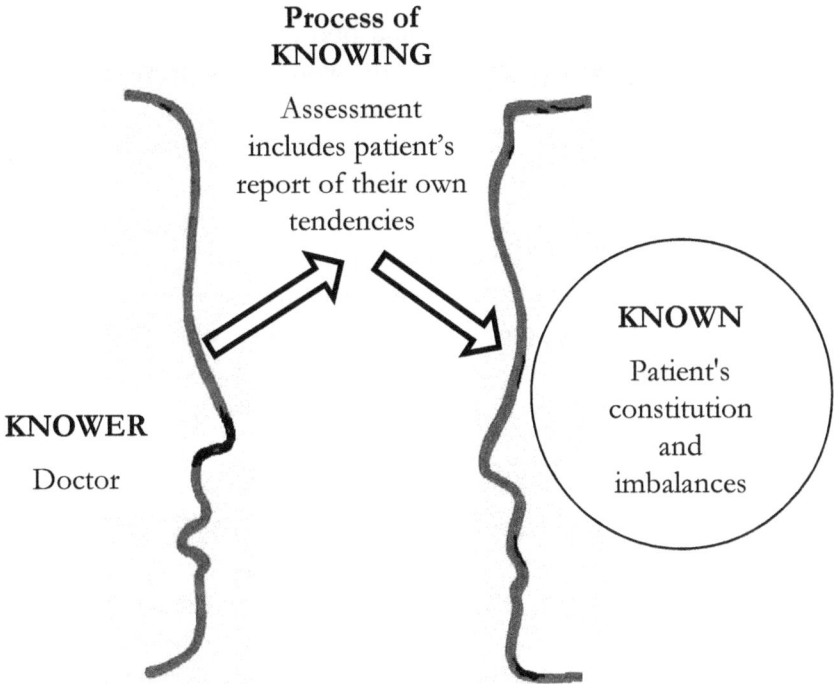

Process of
KNOWING

Assessment
includes patient's
report of their own
tendencies

KNOWER

Doctor

KNOWN

Patient's
constitution
and
imbalances

Doctor-Patient relationship in Natural Medicine

This varies across the different schools and traditions. Some have the specialist in a role similar to Biological Medicine holding secret knowledge. Some use tests which are as hard to understand as Western blood tests. However there is usually more involvement of the patient in the assessment process, taking into account his or her likes and dislikes, habits and tendencies. Some use the person's reactions to substances or pressure. The patient is therefore more part of the process of gaining Knowledge. Some systems are also strong on the patient learning about themselves to be able to better manage their health in the future. They are encouraged to take the Knower role home with them.

Connections to Diversity in Life

Natural medicine does not fit easily into a chart which is structured by the differences between mind and body, individual and environment. This is how modern science sees the world. Natural systems tend to be holistic seeing a unity of life which has different aspects. Natural medicine is best placed in the gaps between mind and body, body and environment. It links the body to the environment through the senses and rhythms in time. The mind and body are linked through postures, breathing and energy techniques.

In Society there is a growing demand for natural therapies and more awareness of the ecology in planning, dealing with pollution etc. We recognise the need for a natural balance in life. Through meditation we see that a more refined mind has more natural desires.

Effectiveness of Natural Medicine in Anxiety

Natural Medicine is most effective if you have high levels of generalised anxiety which are fairly persistent. You have high trait anxiety which is less responsive to Western approaches. High background anxiety is more likely in GAD and Agoraphobia. General anxiety may be high in Social Anxiety if this is fairly widespread not limited to specific situations. Panic Disorder usually means you are prone to anxiety as well as currently being well out of balance.

If the back-ground level of anxiety can be reduced then other specific problems such as phobias or panic or OCD will lessen or be easier to cope with. Natural approaches can be useful adjunctive therapy to other approaches. Some techniques, such as breathing exercises, are also useful for dealing with acute anxiety. Where tension is especially felt is the muscles, massage is obviously useful.

Some forms of natural medicine come from long traditions suggesting there must be truth in them because the knowledge persists. Other forms were dreamed up recently by individuals who may have profound intuitive knowledge but there is less guarantee.

106

Anecdotal reports and advice from friends may be stronger than rigorous double-blind randomised scientific trials which Western medicine prefers. Even Acupuncture which is a highly organised system is criticised in the West for lack of careful enough trials. Many traditions do not fit into the symptom-focussed Western analysis as they look at underlying imbalances or blockages.

For many forms of natural medicine such as aromatherapy, herbs, homeopathy, massage, and music, there are few such trials. There is some positive evidence though often for an immediate effect at the time rather than a lasting benefit. Supporting natural medicine are the traditions, common knowledge on the population and individuals own intuitive sense. Do we need scientific proof to tell us massage is relaxing? We do not but it would be nice to know how effective it was in reducing a long-term tendency to anxiety. Simple regular exercise has been shown to reduce anxiety and also lift mood. There is also some evidence for Yoga exercises.

Among the herbs, aromas and flowers, the Bach Flower Rescue Remedy is a widely used product for panic or fear. Some of its ingredients, Rock Rose and Cherry Plum are also used. Lavender and Chamomile have longer histories of use with some scientific interest in Chamomile. Valerian is popular when a more sedative effect is desired. The best evidenced plant-based material is Kava though this has problems with potential liver toxicity. St John's Wort is well recorded as a depression therapy but also has some effect on anxiety.

Frankincense is a very traditional aroma which has the effect of opening the airways so combatting hyperventilation.

Which people are comfortable with Natural Medicine?

The answer should be everyone as these are natural techniques. The range is so wide that you will naturally favour those that suit your particular constitution and personality. A scientific approach to life may push you towards Western medicine but many people use both approaches. Wealthy and successful people who have resources and choice tend to use both.

Not everyone is keen on talk therapy. Your culture may not see this as appropriate or you may not want to discuss past traumas. The non-verbal techniques of natural medicine may be easier.

The more life-style oriented methods suit you if you are prepared to make some changes. Detox regimes appeal to people who want to enjoy living out of balance and then make up for this later. Other people prefer to have things done to them, with massage and health spas making a come-back in the last 20 years. More refined techniques such as light therapy and energy related methods are more suited to people who are already in a fair state of balance.

Qualities of the mind identified in Natural Medicine

Many traditions do not say much about the nature of the mind as they focus on diet, herbs, massage etc. without a mental component. Often the emphasis is on the mind being affected by the physical body and life-style. Many do hold that the attention of the mind has a positive effect. There is a general belief that the laws of nature underlie the environment and the person but these laws are not necessarily easy to know. Maharishi Ayur Veda holds consciousness to be central to health and this is discussed in the next chapter.

∞ Chapter 8 ∞
Maharishi Ayur Veda – The Science of Life

In recent decades there has been an explosion of new ideas in natural medicine but these therapies are hard to evaluate as they have little context. One of the strengths of traditional systems is that their knowledge has survived thousands of years and this would be unlikely if they were not effective. A therapy dreamed up in California last week does not have this backing.

All countries have their own traditions of natural medicine. The most detailed and widely used traditions are Ayur Veda from India and Traditional Chinese Medicine. There are clear historical links between systems. The four humours were the basis of European medicine for many centuries prior to modern medicine. The humours can be traced back through Greece and the Middle East to the Far East where more comprehensive systems of knowledge were first developed.

Ayur Veda is the oldest tradition of knowledge about health in the world and is recognised by the World Health Organisation. Following Indian independence from British rule there has been a resurgence of traditional knowledge and Maharishi showed how all the areas of Vedic knowledge can be integrated with a science of consciousness. Maharishi Ayur Veda (MAV) describes three basic principles in the physiology called Doshas. These interact to create and run the physiology. The balance of Doshas determines an individual's constitution with one of them, Vata, making you more prone to anxiety imbalance. The same language can be used to describe imbalances. Anxiety disorders are so common because Vata is most easily imbalanced and modern life stresses Vata greatly.

It is obvious that our individual levels of anxiety, mood, weight, and need to sleep vary greatly. MAV recognizes this in terms of our constitutional pattern and uses the same language of the Doshas to describe food and the outside environment, including time. MAV has strong emphasis on diet and daily routines suitable for you as an individual.

MAV sees the body primarily as a pattern of intelligence in communication with consciousness at its basis. This understanding bridges the gap between the physical body, the intelligence of DNA, and underlying laws of nature. In Western science the nervous system in some magical and unknown way supports the experience of consciousness. This gap in understanding should be a major embarrassment. Modern science has increasingly recognized intelligence throughout the body but this intelligence is still distant to that which we experience mentally. Not just the nervous system but the immune, endocrine and digestive systems have rich communication systems. Anxiety is not just felt in the mind but our heart, muscles, and guts all feel anxious too.

The basic interactions of consciousness

For subjective feelings to be more useful we need a better language to link them to advice other than taking of medication. This would allow us to tune our life-style to better balance our own constitutional needs.

Consciousness has some basic modes of activity, like basic frequencies of vibration. This closely parallels the basic elements in quantum field theory. There are a few types of particle and forces which then interact to make up all other sub-atomic pieces and then atoms and so on. MAV describes five elements: earth, water, fire, air and Akasha (space-time). These names give the flavour of the elements but are potentially misleading as these elements are subtle. They also relate to five ways in which consciousness interacts with itself. When these interactions are expressed more superficially they become the five corresponding senses: smell, taste, sight, touch and hearing.

The Three Doshas

The three Doshas contain the five elements in combination. Vata is composed of Akasha and air and so has qualities of lightness and

110

movement. Vata is most associated in the body with rhythms, movement through the circulation, and the nervous system. Pitta is made of fire (and water) so has heat, sharpness and is associated with digestion and metabolism. Kapha is formed of earth and water and supports the structure of the body, fluids and strength. It is character-ised by solidity and connectedness. These principles can be seen at any level. Each cell has its own movement, chemical transformation, and structure. All three are active in our individual constitution but each of us has a different balance. No doubt an individual's constitution also reflects their many individual genes but the language of the Doshas gives a more useful high-level summary of individual tendencies.

DOSHA	ELEMENT	SENSE
VATA	Akasha	Hearing
	Air	Touch
PITTA	Fire	Sight
	Water	Taste
KAPHA	Earth	Smell

Knowing your constitutional type

How can we best know our constitution? This is reflected in our bodily structure and appearance, also in our behavior and preferences. A fair approximation can be made from the following questionnaire in Appendix 1. Circle YES for as many items as seem to apply to you, as you have been for most of your adult life. There are no desirable or better answers. Then add up the number of YES responses in the three columns. This gives a balance of Vata, Pitta and Kapha for your constitution. If one of the three numbers is much higher than the others then this is likely to be your dominant Dosha. For many people

111

two Doshas will be reasonably strong and the third less. For a few, all three Doshas are similar in level of influence.

Another way of determining your constitution is to see an expert in MAV. They would also look at your appearance and ask questions about behavior and likes/dislikes. They take your pulse, as this carries the constitutional balance in it, as well as any temporary imbalance. Best of all is learning to take your own pulse. This strengthens self knowledge. Knowledge of your constitution becomes more direct and your ability to pick up early imbalance more refined. The process of taking your own pulse also provides another self-referral feedback loop between your consciousness and your body. This uses the power of awareness and attention to bring the body back into balance. Pulse diagnosis is beyond the scope of this book and does require practice as well as teaching. It is illustrative of the difference between scientific paradigms that pulse diagnosis is such a prominent part of MAV and also of Traditional Chinese Medicine, yet is completely absent from Western medicine apart from limited information about the heart and circulation.

Once you know your constitution you can use this to guide your choice of diet, exercise and daily routines. For example MAV predicts that when Vata is strong in your constitution, you are more vulnerable to disturbance by caffeine which stimulates Vata greatly often causing anxiety. On the other hand coffee has some settling effect on Pitta and so is traditionally popular in hot countries. You can also take into account the seasonal influences on your physiology. If Vata is strong in your constitution then you are more vulnerable to Vata imbalance. This tendency becomes even stronger in the Vata time of year – typically early winter and fall. At this time especially you can protect yourself by avoiding foods which increase Vata – i.e. cold, raw food, very sour, bitter or astringent food, too little food, irregular meals. This is not to say that you should adopt an extreme diet with none of these. Diet should still be mixed but favouring the other food qualities. In your daily routine, regularity of eating and sleeping will stabilise Vata. Oil massage is also beneficial to Vata as are some aromas like the lavender traditionally grown outside bedroom windows to promote sleep. Appendix 2 gives a summary of the influences on the three Doshas.

Diet has generally been ignored by modern medicine. It was felt that once a person had enough to eat and an adequate vitamin intake little would be gained by varying the diet unless you had a specific digestive problem or were obese. We do have excellent senses of taste and smell and awareness of how full is our stomach. These have all evolved over time, but we have become reluctant to use them or trust them. Indeed it is now commonly assumed that if you really like eating a food it must be bad for you. People often do use food to soothe them-selves but if they use the wrong food they just put on weight or feel dull. Knowing how to relate food to your constitution is the key.

The natural rhythms of life

The internal rhythms of the body reflect or parallel rhythms in the outside world. For seasonal and daily rhythms these are obvious. But why did we decide a week had seven days? It is said God rested on the seventh day after a hard week creating the world. He sent us a reminder in our physiology in our immune and repair systems which have a strong rhythm with a length of seven days. In good health, the different rhythms are well-connected like different sized cog wheels in a clock. Disturbance of rhythm is found to be a major source of imbalance in MAV. This is a great contrast to the culture of many industrialised societies where technology is used to ignore the normal rhythms of life particularly the daily or circadian rhythm. Electricity is a great boon but also allows us to become dissociated from the natural cycles of day and night and the seasons. We avoid mentioning any monthly cycles.

Insomnia

Insomnia troubles over 60 million people in the USA and the costs run into many billions of dollars through direct costs of medical care and the indirect effects on job performance and absenteeism. Anxiety is a common cause of insomnia which then becomes stuck as a problem of rhythm and daily routine. Science has studied circadian rhythms and

113

identified a least two clocks or 24-hour pacemakers in the hypothalamus. Some of the effects of light and dark are known as are mechanisms involving melatonin and amines (the same ones involved in mood). But this knowledge has not led to good cures for insomnia. Drugs provide short-term relief but long-term usually make things worse.

From an Ayur Vedic perspective, insomnia is commonly due to disturbed Vata whose natural tendencies include being fast and variable. Imbalance leads to tiredness or anxiety in the day and variable or poor sleep. Caffeine is a great disrupter of sleep, especially for Vata types. As well as just keeping you awake, coffee also has the effect of weakening the 24 hour internal clock.

Ayur Veda distinguishes between types of insomnia according to the imbalance of the different Doshas. When Vata is the main problem then regularity of routine needs to be emphasised and established. Where Pitta is strong in the constitution, it is important not to go to bed too late. From about 10 p.m. to 2 a.m. Pitta becomes stronger. If you have strong Pitta tendencies and have not gone to bed early enough you may start to feel energised and hungry around this time and describe yourself as a night person, finding it hard to sleep till 1 or 2 a.m. as Pitta reduces. Kapha has characteristics of strength and stability and is less associated with rhythm disturbance. But a person with strong Kapha in their constitution needs to ensure they have long enough hours of sleep and not to disturb their sleep by eating too late in the evening because of the time needed to digest. Exercise will counteract the influence of Kapha and may best be taken during the Kapha time of day such as early evening.

Joanne was a lady in her mid thirties who had suffered much trauma as a child and again in her early adult life. She also had a family history of anxiety and depression. She had always been anxious and led a very restricted life because of her fears for her own safety. These persisted even after she had found a safe person to live with. She had very little social life and was unable to work despite her above average intelligence. Her anxiety levels varied with her mood which swung from OK to very low and her sleep was never good.

114

She had been treated with anti-depressants and mood stabilizing medication which was of some benefit but she still had crises when she required urgent consultations and had been in hospital several times.

Although there were obvious psychological reasons for her anxiety and distress she also had a strong constitutional predisposition with Vata being prominent. Her daily routine was chaotic which had been seen as secondary to her illness. One factor which was overlooked for many years was that she drank many cups of strong coffee a day. She was given advice on daily routine for her Dosha type and strongly counselled to reduce and stop caffeine intake. When she changed her behavior in this way her mood became more even. Her sleep improved and her day-time anxiety reduced significantly. She still had much work to do in psychological therapy but without these simple changes from MAV she would not have been strong enough to undertake this.

Increasing our biological self knowledge

For fine tuning of the physiology or treating of minor conditions, drugs are not so effective. We should understand our own constitution and live a life that complements this. Modern science is not strong in this area and Maharishi Ayur Veda is most useful here.

Awareness extends into the body through our senses. The five major senses correspond to five basic aspects of the material world. As modern science has concentrated on intellectual knowledge of the body as an object it has ignored our physical experience. This is the gap between doctor and patient. The patient feels symptoms while the doctor thinks of a theoretical understanding of molecules, tissues and organs.

An opiate addict has come to have such distorted senses that he feels heroine is good for him. Most of us are not so disturbed. Senses can be trusted, at least a little. This trust can be built on and as consciousness develops our senses refine to become more accurate. We can increasingly determine subjectively what is good for us. The intellect is also useful, but knowledge of chemistry alone will always

115

be incomplete. No matter how many ingredients are listed on a cereal packet, the proof will always be in the eating.

Our senses can be used and should be. They have evolved over the ages and served to connect the deeper levels of the mind of consciousness to the manifest body and outer environment. We naturally know when we are hungry, thirsty, tired, or energetic and can discern in detail what exactly we desire to eat or what type of exercise we enjoy. But we have not cultured these abilities in our education. We do not trust them. Once we are able to trust our senses then we can apply the rule of "Do no harm" directly to ourselves and stop acting or eating in ways that are damaging to health.

Retuning the physiology

This level of intellectual knowledge can be extended by experience. Simply putting attention on the influence of your activity and diet on your body is educational. Everyone has their own unique make-up. The language of the three Doshas allows you to analyse parts of your life in a way that is easier and more practical than the language of chemistry. This analysis always refers back to consciousness. If something makes you feel better with more energy, stability and balance in mind and body then it is likely to be good for you. The effects need to be long-lasting of course. Taking cannabis or alcohol may relieve anxiety for a short while but alcohol makes you more anxious on the rebound and cannabis can precipitate nasty panic or dissociative feelings. Sometimes we crave things short term that we know are bad for us longer term. Usually when this is the case it is better to reduce slowly to avoid discomfort from sudden change and the same is true of changes to daily routine.

It is possible to consult experts in MAV, but the real value of this knowledge is having it in your own mind and developing your own awareness of your state of health. Ayur Veda is almost as wide as modern medicine with different sub-specialties so different Ayurvedic approaches exist. The specific value of the reformulated

From Anxiety To Peace

Maharishi Ayur Veda is that importance is given to consciousness and the deepest principles of Ayur Veda.

Caroline and the MAV Specialist

Caroline is not sure what to expect from the specialist in MAV but the consultation room does smell nice. The specialist asks about disturbances to natural functions like appetite, digestion, sleep and menstruation. He has some interest in her mental disturbance but more in general terms of her feeling fearful and anxious than detailed thoughts. He does want to know about her daily routine and when her problems occur. He does a physical examination − with emphasis on the pulse.

The specialist gives Caroline his assessment of her natural constitution − a mixture of Vata and Pitta. Her current imbalance is mainly in Vata with panic as one result of this. His advice is firstly to improve her diet and daily routine − two pillars of health. This includes regularity of sleep time and reducing mentally stimulating activity in the late evening. Similarly her diet needs to be more regular in timing of eating, without rushing and with a good meal at lunch time. Since it is the Vata season she is also advised to favour Vata-pacifying foods. This all seems a long way from her panic attacks and he gives her a talk on the theory of constitution and the Doshas to make this understandable. There is also further literature and lectures if she wants them.

He further advises her to learn meditation firstly because this has a great benefit on balancing Vata and secondly because of its general effects on health. Establishing calmness deeper in the mind is very protective of being overshadowed by surface anxieties.

There are other specific treatments that could be used for her Vata imbalance. These include herbal medicines, aromatherapy, oil massage, breathing exercises and Yoga asanas. He is aware that Caroline does not want to be overwhelmed and confused. At the

117

second session he discusses some options and she chooses the breathing technique and an oil massage which she can do herself.

MAV acknowledges expertise in the specialist and there are some parallels with the Knower to Known interaction seen in Biological Psychiatry. However there is much more use of the patient's senses. Education is emphasised more to ensure long term balance. The patient becomes the Knower of their own physiology, with the language of MAV to enable this. Many of the interventions are also ones which the patients do for themselves: diet, routine, massage and meditation.

Knower, Knowing and Known in Maharishi Ayur Veda

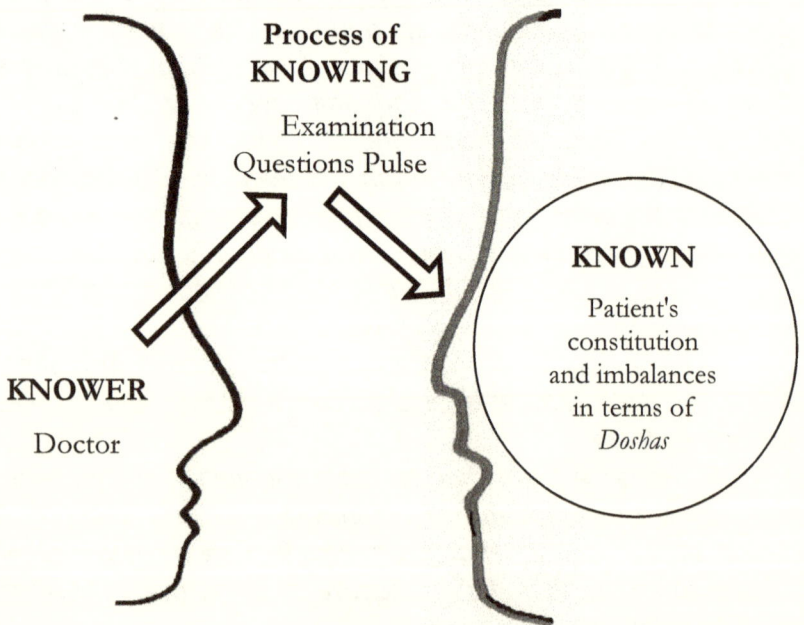

**Process of
KNOWING**

Examination
Questions Pulse

KNOWER

Doctor

KNOWN

Patient's
constitution
and imbalances
in terms of
Doshas

MAV sees the body as much in terms of patterns of intelligence as in material terms. Diet can be analysed as packages of intelligence that relate to the structure of intelligence in our own bodies. Herbal medicines contain information similar to food but in concentrated form. Sensory input also brings information into the system which

118

has an effect on the activity of the nervous system. All these influences may be for better or worse in terms of balance and health.

Connections to the Diversity of Life

MAV does not fit at all easily on a chart with western therapies. This is because the chart was drawn up to include all Western approaches. Western science starts from a world of differences and tries to integrate them. The theory of MAV starts from the unity of natural law and then sees this dividing into the world of differences. A chart for MAV would have the five elements and three Doshas giving rise to the physiology and environment. Both approaches are valid as knowledge has these two directions. Variety comes together in simpler laws and principles. The unity of nature expresses itself in diversity.

The Unified Field as viewed by physics gives rise to a few basic elements of force and matter. In the same way the Unified Field seen from the physiological perspective unfolds as the three Doshas. The five elements are a linking level which can be seen to parallel ideas of the Superstring theory of theoretical physics. Pure consciousness is an infinite homogeneous field. It gives rise to expressed levels and then interacts with these expressions. We experience this in terms of our senses with the main five senses relating directly to the main five paths of expression – the five elements. We are so used to thinking of the world as separate and objective that this may seem supremely simple.

Sharpening the senses

The Unified Field is consciousness. Our experience of consciousness has the same structure as that of the material world. It is only the recent fragmentation of science that has lost track of this truth. If we reclaim this ability then we have direct knowledge of our bodies and the power to keep in a healthier balance.

Just as meditation is a self development technique, MAV has its greatest strength as an educative method. Wellness curricula could include knowledge of your individual constitution as well as the general principles of health. Prevention of disease has not been a

119

strong point for Western medicine other than through immunisation programs. To prevent modern diseases with their internal communication break-downs we need to increase our inner intelligence. The channels for this are our senses and the medium is our conscious experience.

Self-referral is the characteristic of consciousness. This is reflected many-fold in the body. The physiology is replete with feed-back loops, homeostatic mechanisms, and repair processes. If we can establish the most settled state of consciousness in our awareness then we develop our senses down to their finest levels. This will allow us to appreciate the beauties of the outside world more. Closer to home this enables us to feel our physical body, its natural tendencies and any imbalances. As consciousness becomes clearer and more balanced then imbalances in the body become more obvious and can be caught at an earlier stage. The most settled state of consciousness is calm and peaceful, the very opposite of anxiety.

When the body is healthy we feel relaxed and lively. Energy and life flow through our nervous system, our breathing, and our muscles. The normal processes of digestion and sleep seem smooth and satisfying. Health is a very positive experience. The body is in good communication with its deeper levels of intelligence and with the underlying field of our consciousness. The body is a microcosm of creation. It is our privilege to be able to experience every level from the gross to the subtle to the transcendent. This is the range of life described by MAV and experienced by human awareness.

Effectiveness of MAV in Anxiety

As with Natural Medicine in general, MAV is most effective if you have high levels of generalised anxiety, high trait anxiety. High back-ground anxiety and panic attacks mean your constitution is well out of balance with Vata the main suspect.

MAV includes several approaches often used in anxiety: meditation, breathing, oil massage and daily routine. Meditation and massage are seen to immediately move the physiology in the opposite direction to anxiety. Brain wave patterns also settle.

Which people are comfortable with MAV?

People who want to know more about their own nature enjoy the simple language of MAV. People who desire a more balanced life to promote peace find strategies they can easily use. MAV does not need to be complex or require a great deal of time. A few small changes can make a big difference.

Qualities of the mind identified in MAV

∞ Consciousness interacts with itself to give rise to the 5 elements and 5 senses
∞ Our senses can align the intelligence of the body and the environment

∞ Chapter 9 ∞
Transcending to Inner Peace

Meditation comes in many forms. It can start with one of the senses such as sight and go inwards with visualisation. Breathing and relaxation are other entry points. The goal of meditation may be limited to enhancing one quality of mind such as improving your ability to focus. More profound meditations go for expansion of the mind itself and experience of deeper levels of consciousness. My preference is for Transcendental meditation (TM). This is an easy to learn method which has been shown to be very effective in anxiety and has other health benefits.

In cognitive and hypnotic schools, reality reflects the content of attention, the content of conscious awareness. The world is as we are, as we think it is. Some forms of meditation use attention as their main strategy. These include concentration, forcing the attention to stay on a candle for example, and contemplation where the attention is allowed to wander a bit but around one topic. This could be a quality you wish to strengthen such as love, compassion or calmness. These techniques may enhance your ability to focus attention and still the mind somewhat. They are less likely to lead to expansion of awareness because attention is being directed to some point on the surface in the world of differences. Such a practice can help with focusing and concentrating, but does not allow the mind to go deeper. Contemplation does allow the mind to move to different associations but these tend to be linked by the intellect and meanings. Again this keeps the mind on or near its surface in the world of differences.

The mind, which seems to be lost in diversity, can rediscover the unity of experience in consciousness. On the surface of the mind, the Knower, Knowing, and Known seem to be very separate. Our thoughts are like objects, separate from the self who is observing them. Transcendental Meditation is an easy technique that uses a special thought, a sound or mantra from the Vedic tradition. The

123

particular function of this thought is that it allows the awareness to entertain it at deeper and deeper levels. This occurs easily because deeper levels of the mind are attractive. The most attractive level is the deepest, transcendental level, the origin and unified basis of all thoughts. Often, this experience of transcendental consciousness seems familiar, like a memory. It is naturally familiar to us as it is not foreign, but just our Self, aware of itself in its expanded state.

This process of meditation is not concentration, nor contemplation. You experience deeper levels of the mind before intellectual knowledge at those levels is available to us. TM is easy, because it is a technique of direct experience. No special belief, understanding, or education is needed to start. It uses the natural process of thinking, which we all possess.

When pure consciousness is experienced in meditation, its qualities start to be infused into activity outside of meditation. These qualities include energy, creativity, and intelligence. These are experienced by a meditator and can be validated by scientific research. Core intelligence and creativity are usually difficult to improve. Practice of TM has been shown to improve them consistently, unfolding inner potential. In the body also, biological intelligence and healing are strengthened.

With regular experience of consciousness at its transcendental level, not only the qualities, but also the experience of pure consciousness remains when our mind comes out of meditation into active lives of diversity.

Pure consciousness - the source of thought

TM has its primary goal as allowing the mind to be in its most settled state. In TM the attention is allowed to go to deeper and expanded experience. This is a dialectic experience as deeper levels of the mind do permit the coexistence of opposites. Restfulness and alertness are both found in pure awareness, stability and adaptability, focus and wide comprehension.

Stability of emotions and experiencing unchanging consciousness to support the realms of change are benefits of TM. Changing

124

emotions are part of life's rich pageant but they cannot be fully enjoyed if life itself is overwhelmed by them. Being established in Transcendental Consciousness (TC) allows us to construct greater emotions because the foundations of the mind are more secure.

TC is that level of the mind that needs no external validation as it is self-validating. It underlies everything else, so nothing is truly external to it. Pure consciousness is aware of itself and validates itself, a blissful experience which is the opposite of emotional distress. As does the Unified Field of physics, pure consciousness contains creativity, flexibility and discrimination.

TM and Behavioral principles - being at home with your Self

In order to practise more settled states of mind we need a reliable technique. Simple relaxation, listening to music, gardening etc. will achieve some calming effect. However these do not reliably achieve the expanded consciousness of which we are capable. TM is a simple practice to unfold this potential. It allows the mind to experience deeper levels of itself. This allows more knowledge and ability to blossom. Even though it is a mental technique it uses behavioral strategies. It is primarily a technique of experience rather than of analysis. Regular practice is the key instruction. Intellectual skills and theoretical understanding are not necessary, though as experience develops knowledge may naturally be sought.

TM certainly uses positive reinforcement. The reason that the attention can and does dive inwards so easily is that deeper levels of the mind are more powerful and creative and more restful. This restful alertness is most attractive and rewarding. When the mind transcends all relative levels to experience its basic level of pure awareness, this is an experience of bliss. Repeated practice gives more familiarity with deeper levels and shapes the process of meditation by rewarding deeper experiences more. The qualities of restfulness becoming stabilised in activity is very much akin to the behavioral technique of associating relaxation with specific activity such as being in a phobic situation.

Transcending to Inner Peace

Because deeper levels are more rewarding, transcending is also a process of shaping. Repeated practice leads to experiencing deeper and deeper levels more frequently and more fully. In TM we experience restful alertness and more settled consciousness in the 20 minutes of practice. These qualities of consciousness then become more available and established in daily activity outside of meditation. One complaint in Agoraphobia is not feeling safe, hence staying at home in a safe place. With TM, a sense of inner peace and security grows. Established in a state of TC you feel absolutely at home with yourself and this is not overshadowed by external situations.

In a scientific age where trust is low, scientific evidence of concrete results may be more appealing than ancient traditions. These show benefits from experiencing TC of increased restfulness, reduced anxiety, reduced unhealthy behaviors like addiction. Impulsiveness is reduced, allowing higher functions more control over behavior. Enjoyment of life increases through enhancement of the natural reward mechanism.

Behaviorism also suggests that activity is necessary to gain reinforcement and reward. The practice of TM involves reducing activity in one sense, sitting with the eyes closed, but increasing it in another, because deeper levels of the mind are more powerful and have more energy. The deepest level of the mind, pure consciousness, is a state of little outer activity with mental experience in its most settled state. But the terrific dynamism inherent in this level is experienced as liveliness and reverberating bliss. Pure consciousness is its own reinforcer. However, the mind does not get stuck in this bliss because there is also creativity and a desire to be more active. The nervous system is by nature an active system. Consciousness desires to express itself and wishes to display its qualities of creativity, intelligence, and bliss in activity. We come out of meditation to enjoy daily life even more.

Silence and Dynamism in Transcendental Consciousness

The simplest and most successful method of BT has been to associate relaxation and calm with previously distressing or phobic situations. We

From Anxiety To Peace

can then be active, e.g. entering a phobic situation, and at the same time retain an inner peace. If this is taken further we can see an ideal life as being able to have unshakable inner stillness at the same time as any dynamic activity. This is possible because TC has these two opposing qualities, silence and dynamism, simultaneously.

BT sees growth and learning as driven by the increasing happiness of being rewarded. The pursuit of happiness is natural and automatic, as is the pursuit of higher and higher goals. The ultimate destination of this journey is complete happiness in our mind, often called bliss. Intelligence is one key quality of consciousness. Bliss is another. TC underlies all our intelligence at more superficial levels. It also supports all relative levels of happiness.

Mary was a practical lady who enjoyed teaching. She had not generally been anxious but found illness difficult. In her fifties she had breast cancer. This responded well to therapy. Mentally she did not respond so well. She found the uncertainty of not knowing if she would stay in remission very hard. She was not well placed to think about the end of her life, whenever that might be. She became anxious, unable to focus on activity and she ruminated on worries about her health.

She learned TM on the advice from a friend and started with no great expectations. She took to it easily and soon found her mind became calmer and less troubled. Her natural concerns about her health remained but were no longer over-shadowing. She regained an interest in spirituality which she had left behind in her teens. Her clear experience of life at a level finer than the physical enabled her to appreciate more the value both of her own life and of her friends.

Transcendental Meditation and Cognitive Therapy

Consciousness is primary in Vedic science. The quality of life we experience reflects the qualities of consciousness expressed and the contents of conscious awareness. The deeper levels of the mind are more encompassing and more powerful just as deeper levels of physics described more powerful levels nature. Sub-atomic forces are more powerful than the chemical. At the basis of the mind is pure consciousness which is infinitely powerful and blissful. This explains why deeper levels of the mind support a more positive mood. They are closer to bliss and resonate more closely this quality of pure consciousness. Deeper levels of the mind therefore reflect both stronger intellectual powers and more blissful mood.

Maharishi's Vedic science also teaches the two steps of progress, knowledge and experience. In CT, knowledge is applied through home-work then new thinking is practised and results analysed. Similarly with the development of higher states of consciousness through Vedic science, this alternation is useful and should have observable results. Through our own subjective experience and the systematic scientific study of others, we can validate the benefits of the growth of consciousness. In our own journey we experience more of the deeper levels of consciousness and this leads to a greater ability to seek intellectual understanding of the inner world. In turn this supports further growth of experience.

Experience is primary in transcending

The ability to observe your surface thinking patterns and then to change them requires awareness to go to a more abstract level. This is exactly what TM means, a meditation process of transcending to deeper levels of awareness. Intellectual abstraction allows some standing back and going beyond. But this is a difficult process to pursue to the deepest levels of the mind. The intellect is not clever enough to comprehend all the complexities and inter-relatedness in life. This is why the process of TM is primarily one of experience. The fundamental levels of the mind are experienced first, with intellectual knowledge following.

Allowing creativity and intelligence to unfold

The benefits of TM include the growth of intelligence which is hard to achieve otherwise, the growth of problem solving, better memory, and focus. But these benefits are automatic following on from the growth of consciousness; they are not the primary methods of growth. Transcending also frees up imagination and creativity. Creative thoughts are commonly experienced as being deeper, as coming from within us.

128

Pure consciousness is the source of all thoughts and by nature it is creative.

Indeed, from the level of pure consciousness only life-supporting thoughts will arise. To develop this potential we need the right to education and training. TM is a basic strategy for this. CT makes use of our natural ability to think. Likewise for TM, the only ability needed it that of thinking. We can all think and thinking at more settled levels is easy. Thinking is a core human ability. Transcending beyond thought to pure consciousness at the source of all thoughts is also part of our birth-right and one we need to claim. TC is just the end state of the process of transcending where awareness has transcended all levels of thought and is left reflecting only on itself. More advanced programs such as the TM Sidhi program deal with culturing the ability to promote thought from the finest level of the mind.

TM and Psychoanalysis

Despite being a "depth psychotherapy" Freudian analysis does not think much of the transcendental field. It is preoccupied with differences. Freud found his patients did not achieve insight at all easily. Their resistance was strong. Some of his later writing became more pessimistic as he contemplated man having a naturally negative side preventing recovery. In this respect Freud failed to use his own principles. He failed to find a deeper and more significant level of the mind. Instead he proposed a negative or death instinct counter-acting the life supporting instinct, libido. He persisted in seeing the mind as being constructed of parts in conflict with each other.

Vedic science extends the principles of Psychoanalysis. Our consciousness does extend beyond the surface to more powerful levels and certainly beyond the waking state. Several other states of consciousness exist beyond waking and dreaming states. Maharishi's Vedic science locates the deepest level of the mind, a concept not seen in analysis, though suggested later in Self realisation. Again, knowledge and experience are both recognized as being necessary. It is the experience of TC, consciousness in its simplest state, which

129

brings an entirely new element to help resolve conflicts. Without this, blocks are hard to overcome at their own level. Freud found conflicts and blocks in the deeper levels of the mind, but could not locate the layer beneath these. He failed to advance his mental science to the extent that physical sciences were able to move. Physics found quantum fields and then the Unified Field underlying the world of material differences. Freud's mechanics remained fixated at the stage of classical physics.

Vedic science agrees with the reciprocity between inner and outer worlds. It extends this idea to cover not just personal relationships but also the physical environment, as all the laws of nature are found in the Unified Field of consciousness, not just those concerning human interactions. Regarding separation, this is only apparent in the surface layers of life and the more expressed levels of the mind. At the depth, there is no separation, pure consciousness being a common source and place of unity. The goal of growth is not just to tolerate separation or reach compromise, but to fully experience all levels of the mind to find unity and bliss. Enlightenment is our goal. Here both unity and separation can co-exist.

Maharishi's Vedic Science agrees on the need for a good doctor to be a healthy doctor, ideally an enlightened person. This concept is surprisingly absent from modern medicine, even in psychiatry. The doctor telling you to give up drugs and alcohol may not have followed his own advice. Addiction rates are higher in doctors then in most professions. A healthy doctor is needed not just to set a good example, but also to tolerate the imbalance or stress in the patient. Fulfilling Rogers' requirements, to honestly have positive regard and accurate empathy for all disturbed states, are a fair test for enlightenment. This is a supremely positive and generous state of mind not shaken by any turbulence.

Integration of thought and feeling is best achieved from the level of mind where both have their source. This is easier than endless complex negotiations between the two at a more superficial level. Their commonality lies at the transcendental level. This is also the basis of all states of consciousness. To fully comprehend both dreaming and waking is impossible in either of these changing relative states. Both are expressions of the same underlying field of pure consciousness, both are shadows of the same sun.

We can also gain greater unity of mind through experience rather than analysis of knowledge. This is the Vedic strategy which goes for experience of the deepest level of the mind first. As TC is so attractive, the mind will go for this, given the chance with TM. Experience of TC occurs quite quickly. On the basis of this profound experience, knowledge and experience of intermediate levels becomes much easier. Psychoanalysis is more akin to a laborious archaeological dig in which each layer is examined from the surface downwards. Many brilliant minds have toiled away in the different schools and announced many treasures, but they have lacked a technique for easily experiencing the most valuable levels of reality.

As the mind dives in meditation through its own layers, this does involve the intellect in discriminating different levels of consciousness, but it is driven by the heart in pursuit of happiness and bliss. The results of experiencing more pure consciousness naturally include more happiness in everyday life. Depression and negative emotions are less, stability of mood greater. Also improved are higher abilities such as moral reasoning and creativity. This growth is not a selfish one. Personal relationships improve in the family and the workplace. More love is felt because more love flows from the transcendental feeling of unity with others. TC is the field of unity beneath the outer world of separateness.

So the mind has deeper layers which are all within consciousness and the transcendental level of consciousness has aspects of being the Self and of being beyond individuality. Jung recognized synchronicity, a non-causal connecting principle. Again this points to the relatedness of people, things, and events through an underlying linkage in the field of intelligence that is not yet open to our awareness.

Psychoanalysis tends to discover the small self, and to promote selfish goals. In concentrating on our own problems there is a drift to moral relativism. Later schools of analysis grew beyond selfishness by either emphasising the positive value of other people or looking to the more transcendental values within. Analysis has been accused of

131

promoting moral relativism, depending on your own values whatever they might be. Even if analysis has helped undermine more widely held moral and spiritual values, it still supports a basic instruction not to do what you know to be wrong.

Freud underestimated the capacity for the waking state, our normal awareness in the day, to be extended. The conscious mind can be broadened and deepened. There are more profound levels of the mind available to us. Dreaming is a different state of consciousness. When we dream we are not without consciousness, but are conscious in a different style of functioning. Some of the processes in the dreaming state of consciousness are found in deep levels of waking consciousness. But the majority of these deeper levels are quite different to dreaming. The deepest layers of consciousness underlie both waking and dreaming states. The conscious mind is not a boat floating in a sea of unconsciousness. The whole sea is consciousness. Its depths are realms of profound intelligence which become comprehensible to the waking mind as it grows.

TM and Biology

Every state of consciousness has its own physiology. Waking, dreaming, and sleeping all have their own corresponding styles of functioning for the nervous system. This can easily be measured in the brainwaves as well as through the pulse, breathing, muscle activity and hormones. The experience of TC is another state of consciousness which also has its own style of physiology. Dr Wallace first detailed the characteristics of a deeper rest than sleep accompanied by greater wakefulness. Looking at the surface levels in the body we see reduced heart rate, blood pressure and muscle relaxation etc. At a chemical level we see hormonal and metabolic changes that are the opposite of stress. The neurophysiology shows more stability and faster recovery of balance. In the EEG the brain shows increased alpha and theta power and coherence of activity across many parts of the brain. Every state of consciousness has its corresponding state of physiological functioning. As the mind gains rest it is able to release or recover from the effects of stress. A less stressed

From Anxiety To Peace

nervous system is clearer and able to support a more refined level of consciousness.

As the transcendental values of consciousness start to endure alongside waking, dreaming, and sleeping, so the physiology of those states also start to benefit. The increased restfulness reverses the effects of stress and to a significant extent the effects of ageing. The body is able to respond faster and also recover quicker after activity. The natural rhythms of the body become stronger. Rest and happiness are powerful treatments for stress. When the body can maintain the quality of restfulness and the mind maintains bliss, stresses are resolved as soon as they are incurred. This explains why an enlightened person can be more dynamic than previously. Another way of looking at this is that the stability and unchanging nature of the transcendent better allows us to tolerate change which is so natural to the surface level of life.

Vedic science finds agreement with modern science regarding the body being structured in layers. There is also agreement that these are layers of intelligence which are dynamic and interactive. Vedic science finds the mind and body affect each other at every level, but their fundamental connection is at the most basic level of our intelligence. Subjectively this is our most settled state of consciousness. Objectively we look down to finer and finer levels of the material world until we run into the Planck Scale below which level there is only intelligence and the laws of nature. This is the realm of the Unified Field in physics. Biology has stopped or paused at the chemical level of DNA. It needs to go deeper to see that because the Unified Field and TC are one the basis of the mind and the body is the same field.

If it is possible for us to experience an underlying field of consciousness through TM, and if this field also forms the basis of our physiology, we might expect that practising meditation would benefit health in many areas, not just those thought to be stress-related. Orme-Johnson's study in 1978 finds exactly this. He compares health insurance data for 2000 meditators compared to other clients with the same insurance programme. He showed that essentially all classes of illness reduced as measured by healthcare utilisation. The equality

133

of use for obstetric care suggests that this was not due to some sub-cultural avoidance of health services. For diseases whose risk factors are known some fascinating additional results are available. Heart disease has some well-known risk factors including smoking, high blood pressure, cholesterol, reactivity to stress, and hostility. All of these individual factors are reduced in TM practitioners. This strongly suggests that a deeper and more comprehensive level of intelligence is being used which effects many areas of the mind, body and behavior. This is a health promoting technique rather than a treat-ment. The natural state of the body is health and balance. TM promotes the power of own homoeostatic and healing processes in both mind and body.

For anxiety the physiology changes in the opposite direction and trait anxiety is reduced over time. Addictive behaviors lessen and mood becomes more stable. There is more inner control or field independence.

Group Consciousness

The existence of group consciousness is well acknowledged in Vedic science. The whole is more than the sum of the parts. In group therapy we can experience the consciousness of a small group of people united in a common task. Our awareness is not usually open to collective consciousness on a grander scale. Vedic science sees collective consciousness as the basis of individual consciousness - it is not just generated by individuals. This is directly parallel to individual particles being expressions of an infinitely wide quantum field. From this perspective individual health is dependent on group health and one member of the family will definitely struggle to be fully healthy if the family is sick.

These are many characteristics of TC indicated by group therapy. Firstly the group is greater than the sum of individual members. The reality of the underlying field of consciousness is much more than all the parts of an individual mind or even than the sum of all individual minds. It is unbounded. Secondly the level of collective conscious-ness can support transformation in an individual. Coherence and life-supporting influence from the wider field of consciousness has a direct effect on us as separate people. We are embedded in the larger field of consciousness which is transcendental. Consciousness has self-referral as its defining quality. This is the basis of its self-sufficiency. The mutual interactions within a group reflect the self-interactive properties of the group consciousness. Daniel Bohm, a physicist, suggests that open dialogue can use the experience of group consciousness to discover the underlying field of consciousness.

Evidence can be seen in the improved personal relationships of meditators in their families and in their places of work. They have an increasingly positive influence on others and live in greater coherence with each other. This may be partly due to better communications, sensitivity and interpersonal relationships. However, because they have increased coherence at a transcendental level, the most important dynamics are at this level. This can be clearly seen when a large group of people meditate together and even more so if they practice the advanced TM Sidhi programme. The interaction between individuals in this group generates sufficient coherence to radiate outside the group at an unseen level in the transcendence of collective consciousness. Research shows this effect improves the quality of collective life and reduces problems such as crime.

Transcendental Consciousness and Natural Medicine

TC contains all the information about the mind, body, and environment. Living in harmony with the outside natural world can be enhanced by having our awareness open to TC. This level of consciousness cannot be unbalanced even though the material nervous system which supports our individual experience can of course be affected. The more our physical body is aligned with its own underlying intelligence in consciousness, the more resistant to stress and ill-health it becomes. The experience of TC has its own physiological state of restful alertness. At this transcendental level, consciousness is its own physiology. The structure and functioning of intelligence at this level are the same. The potential for imbalance seen in the material field of diversity is no longer possible here.

135

The laws of nature are multiple and complex, whether seen through the eyes of modern science of many natural systems. The advantage of knowledge at the level of TC is that it is naturally compacted and integrated. This makes it possible to live in harmony with natural law even though we do not know all the individual laws intellectually. From a transcendental perspective, the splitting of knowledge into separate pieces is the mistake which ultimately leads to a life out of balance and a loss of unity of consciousness.

Meditation educates the mind to experience a level of pure awareness. As we use its qualities in activity our inner potential is unfolded. Latent abilities and knowledge within our consciousness come out. The simplest one is the ability to be restful even in dynamic activity. Within the field of TC we find its structure to be the laws of nature. This is why familiarity with this level makes us so at home with the laws of nature. As these laws underlie and govern the environment we naturally feel more at home in any situation. Self-knowledge and knowledge of the environment become integrated.

Caroline learns TM

Caroline is keen to learn TM but a bit anxious as she has found it hard to relax or settle her mind down in the past. After a couple of explanatory talks she is taught the technique quite quickly and practises on her own for 20 minutes twice a day. She goes back for follow up sessions on the next three days. She is surprised that meditation is so easy. Within a few days TM has become a natural part of her daily routine. Besides enjoying a good rest during the practice time she notices that her sleep improves within a week and she feels more alert and clear in the day. Over the next few weeks her general confidence improves and she feels less inclined to avoid situations that previously made her anxious. Without really knowing why she feels less worried about things and several people tell her she looks happier. Over the next months she has some very pleasant peaceful experiences in meditation though nothing flash. In her activity she continues to grow stronger and feel more at home with herself whatever each day brings. This is experienced as a natural and welcome progression.

Enlightenment is the profound cure for Caroline's panic as we learn from the Upanishads: "Who sees all beings in his own Self, and his own Self in all beings, loses all fear."

Knower, Knowing and Known in Transcendental Meditation

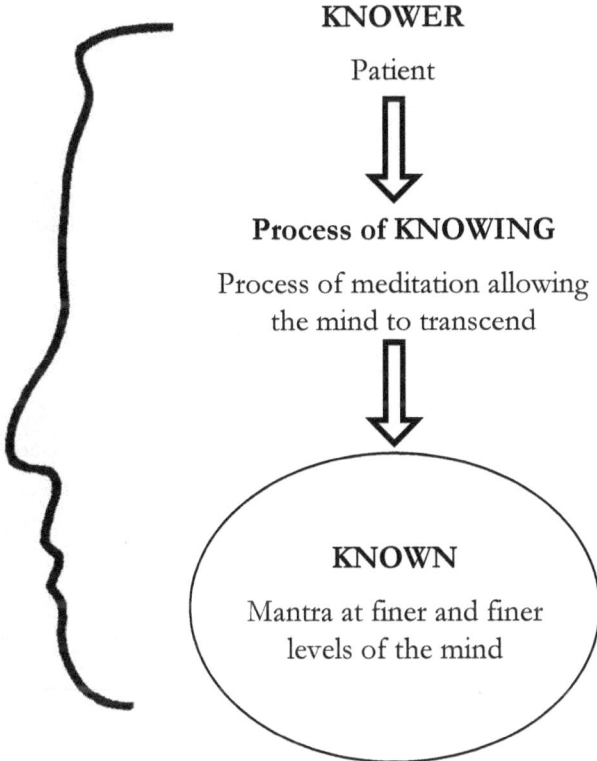

KNOWER

Patient

⇓

Process of KNOWING

Process of meditation allowing
the mind to transcend

⇓

KNOWN

Mantra at finer and finer
levels of the mind

137

Doctor-Patient Relationships in TM

TM does need to be learned from a trained teacher as it is a subtle process. Once learned it is practised at home with no teacher present. The Knower - Knowing - Known relationships are all in the Patient's own mind. As the attention travels to the deeper levels, the Knower, Knowing, and Known (mantra) become both more refined and closer together. As the attention dives into the transcendental, the three become one, and consciousness is aware of itself, an experience of pure consciousness on its own. This is an experience of the simplest state of consciousness.

Effectiveness of TM in Anxiety

During the practice of TM the body becomes very rested with lower pulse, blood-pressure, and breathing. Hormones associated with stress reduce. When the mind experiences pure consciousness in TM, which is the polar opposite of feeling anxious, the body also is at its most settled with breathing becoming extremely settled and the EEG becoming coherent across the brain with the lower frequency alpha and theta waves strengthening.

The results outside of meditation are cumulative over time. This is unlike most other courses of therapy where results tend to taper off once the initial learning phase is over. In particular, trait anxiety reduces over time. A meta-analysis showed this effect for TM was greater than for other relaxation techniques. TM has been shown to lead to a spontaneous reduction in smoking, alcohol, illegal drug and caffeine use which are all signs of stress. Several studies find that personality characteristics improve which are usually hard to shift such as self realisation, cooperativeness, and moral reasoning. These may be seen as signs of increasing maturity. TM is seen to work at the deeper level of the constitution and personality. It has been less studied in specific anxiety disorders. There are a number of studies in hard to treat groups such as prisoners and people with addiction.

Which people are comfortable with TM?

As TM is an easy and natural technique it can be learned by anyone. Prior knowledge or belief is unnecessary. As with BT it works if you just do it. In fact, scepticism is a very healthy attitude because you are then likely to make no effort in the practice and this is just the right way to practise TM. No great intelligence is required. You only need to be able to follow some simple instructions and TM has been learned by people with intellectual handicap. Children under 10 years old learn in a modified form as they are not inclined to sit with their eyes closed for 20 minutes.

TM does not interfere with other therapies and can be used alongside another course of treatment from a doctor or psychologist. TM does not present itself just as a treatment. It is more of a self-development or educational approach. It therefore appeals to people who want to improve themselves or who believe they have not reached their potential. It may be learned for specific psychological reasons, to reduce anxiety or improve sleep, but the benefits will be wide including physical health and relationships.

Qualities of the mind identified in TM

∞ The mind goes naturally to deeper levels
∞ These levels are more restful but also more alert
∞ The most settled state of mind is simply pure consciousness aware of itself

Transcending to Inner Peace

∞ Chapter 10 ∞
Being Fully Awake and at Peace

Anxiety disorders are currently very prevalent and minor worries and distress even more common. The situation for mental health today is similar to that of physical health in the Middle Ages, at least in Europe. In this colourful time physical health was extremely poor and life expectancy short. Among the major contributors to this were a lack of clean water and good sewerage systems. Levels of personal hygiene were low. People and their domestic environments were very dirty by modern standards. Because everybody was unclean this would not have seemed abnormal. Today it is the general level of mental hygiene that is low. The average person has a great deal of stress and disturbance in their mind. Because that is the common situation it does not appear unusual and distress is seen as a normal part of the human condition. Future centuries will look back on our time as being as mentally muddy as the Middle Ages were physically dirty.

In physical health we recognize that physical fitness also encompasses extending strength, stamina and flexibility. We want to use more of our physical potential. The same should be true in mental health. Excellent mental health should be the normal adult state. This includes not just peace of mind but also meaningful and successful personal relationships and roles in society. It should include the fulfillment of our role in the universe, our spiritual life. These are all within our human potential but, just as for physical fitness, this potential is often not realised.

We enjoy technological progress and now live in the age of information. Material science is growing so fast that we cannot even predict the technologies that will be in common use in a few years time. We may worry about how to program our smart phones. The real concern is that we have not mastered the technology of our own consciousness. Only the human animal has evolved to enjoy pure consciousness. From the developmental perspective, mental health means maturing to enjoy what evolution has already delivered to us.

141

Self knowledge is all

In order to improve our mental health we must have more knowledge. Primarily we require knowledge about ourselves. This includes learning new habits and extending our mental and intellectual capacity. We can expand our conscious awareness to overcome conflicts and blocks in our emotions which were previously unconscious. We need to understand our own physical body in a language which is meaningful and can be used to guide our daily life. Sharpening our senses will give us better feedback about the state of our physical health and the influence of the physical environment. Other people who make up our social environment can become more familiar and more intimate to us.

Every one of these levels of self knowledge can be approached individually and the different psychological approaches provide useful strategies and inspiration. Behavior therapy shows how easily we can overcome our phobias. Cognitive theory shows how our conscious thinking process structures our experience of reality. Analysis looks to make the unconscious mind more available to the waking state, to integrate thinking and feeling. Group processes link the individual with a wider mental system. These levels of mind all exist within our consciousness. All have as their basis the field of consciousness and we are able to experience this field in its simplest and purest state. Familiarity with this level of the mind supports and strengthens all other levels. Efforts towards self knowledge in all the relative areas of life will be more fruitful. In addition we are able to gain knowledge of the larger transcendental Self which is truly Self realisation. The mind becomes fully awake as the silent field of pure consciousness remains lively even in the midst of a noisy activity.

Diversity is the nature of life in all its multi-coloured expressions. In this garden of diversity, health is characterised by balance and harmony. The different elements of intelligence giving rise to our constitution are in balance with each other and in harmony with the environment. The internal rhythms of our body are in time with the natural cycles created by the earth's movement in the solar system. Our thoughts and feelings can be integrated. Individual desires and the agendas of others are synchronised. Coherence between different

142

parts create a wholeness which not only functions better, it can start working on a new and higher plane. When all levels of the mind become integrated, then enlightenment dawns and our quality of mental life improves radically. When individuals work together coherently, our family and national life are transformed.

Unhealthy behaviors which we have accumulated can be unlearned and forgotten. We can educate and train ourselves and our children to remember our full potential. By remembering the Unified Field of intelligence we overcome the mistake of the intellect which was to become overshadowed by diversity. We can recognize this mistake intellectually. By allowing our awareness to transcend we can directly experience the reality of unity within consciousness. Fragmentation and separation are the key features of individual illness and social problems. Any cure must be in the direction of more coherence. Maintaining unity in our own conscious experience is a powerful method of promoting and maintaining health.

Choosing a route to peace

The most important step to peace and enlightenment is the first one. You need to accept that the journey is possible. Even if the goal looks far away a start can be made. This is a good lesson from cognitive therapy. When you are beset by anxieties it seems hard to go forward and helplessness sets in. But progress can still be made, as you are never truly helpless. Much of the damage done by our fears is done by our reaction to them. If you are unable to change them, then just accepting they are present and not over-reacting can free you up to begin taking back control of your life.

We have seen the many paths towards peace and you may need to travel along more than one. You need to know your starting point. This includes what sort of anxiety disorder you have. Are you generally an anxious person? What is your life-style?

One of the timeless rules of medicine is that a doctor should first do no harm, Prima non nocere. We should apply the same advice to our own activity. If we are repeatedly doing something we know to be aggravating anxiety, then we must take steps to decrease

Being Fully Awake and at Peace

and stop. We should not accept this as an inevitable part of who we are. No one is by nature a heavy coffee drinker. Coffee increases anxiety and disrupts sleep. Alcohol is soothing for a short period but anxiety is worse on the rebound. Cannabis can also be attractive but triggers panic and nasty dissociated states. By nature we are all people who can change and learn. We can change our habits and learn to live healthier lives and so evolve to a less anxious life. We can put our attention on behavior we wish to change. Simply recording and monitoring behavior focuses our attention. This creates a feedback loop between consciousness and behavior. We can look at the consequences of our actions and check if these are in line with our goals in life. Were we given the gift of a human nervous system so we could sedate it with alcohol and pep it up with caffeine?

Habits of health

Habits and behaviors are simple parts of everyday life. But they have powerful effects on us because they form the structure of our life and their consequences determine our future. Healthy routines and especially daily routines of sleeping eating and exercising are major foundations of a stronger constitution. Meditation is a part of daily routine that serves as a deep rest, a mental bath and mental exercise. These habits will improve the ride whatever other paths we travel on.

Increasing confidence

If your anxiety is a Specific Phobia then Behavioral Therapy is the recommended route. It is fast and effective. It can be done individually or in groups. Which you choose will depend on availability, possibly cost as groups are cheaper, and your preference.

Social Phobia also calls for a behavioral approach but there is likely to be a cognitive element so CBT is the answer. Again, individual or group therapy is possible but there is a special advantage for groups here because the group itself provides a situation in which to grow in social confidence.

Panic disorder often needs more than one approach with breathing retraining and cognitive therapy for catastrophic thinking

144

being main choices. Medication can be effective short to medium term. Where Agoraphobia is present, CBT is advised to ensure you regain your confidence in activity. For OCD also a combination of CBT and medication is usual for more severe illness.

Generalised Anxiety Disorder is better seen as an anxiety trait. Education about the nature of anxiety and just monitoring yourself are the simplest steps of cognitive and behavioral approaches and these are recommended for mild cases. You can progress to more intensive psychological therapy or medication if needed. However this is often seen as a resistant or chronic condition when treated as an illness. Better is to balance your "nervous" constitution with meditation, attention to lifestyle, and natural medicine techniques. These include the important attention to daily routine, diet and exercise. Breathing techniques and massage are especially used but there are choices from the other senses.

If you have one of the more specific disorders such as Social Phobia but are also generally anxious, then you can use the specific approach of BT for the Social Phobia and the more general approaches for GAD.

When you know that your problems can be traced back to some prior life events such as child-hood abuse, you may want to back-track to sort out your emotions around these experiences. This requires a good therapist so do not settle for a generic counsellor. Analytic therapy is a tougher road and it may be best to prepare for it by using some of the general approaches to get your-self in good shape. If you have great difficulty tolerating distress your therapy may need to start with learning some simple CBT techniques before delving onto the past.

If you have a poor opinion of therapists and experts then self-help groups could be for you. These groups can combine elements of therapy, social support and opportunities to regain confidence in a safer environment.

You will feel most comfortable if you understand the therapy you are using, how it works, how long it takes, and what the goal of therapy is. Reading this book will have given you guidance about the main choices. It is still best to discuss with a doctor or therapist to

145

check you are in agreement. A good doctor should also be able to discuss the options of other therapies, though of course they will have some bias to their own method.

We have seen how different therapies use and develop the Knower, Knowing or Known values in a patient. If you are happy to remain only the Known or object of study then Biological psychiatry is for you. But do make some effort to capture a bit of the Knower role through educating yourself and improving your life-style.

If you seek more of the Knower position, consider exactly what you want to know. To know your own biology more intimately you should try natural medicine and particularly Maharishi Ayur Veda with its use of the senses and of consciousness. BT gives knowledge of simple action steps to reduce symptoms and avoidance behavior without a great deal of talk or detailed theory. To be master of your thinking process, Cognitive Therapy is the key. It is more wordy as it uses the process of Knowing itself as a medium for therapy. To unlock the secrets of your past and emotions a more analytic therapy is needed. To know your Self, take to meditation with the easiest and best researched option being TM. To know God – that is beyond this book but sorting out your anxiety state may still be a place to start.

You may be happy to learn in more than one way, to discuss and find your way forward with others. Self-help groups can give you this flexibility. Here you are more in charge of the process of learning. CT is also strong in this aspect as you take control of your process and patterns of thinking.

Enlightenment as normal maturity

The standard expected from mental health is already rising and can be raised even further. Normal maturity means achieving the potential that human evolution already provides. This means that education and upbringing include much more development of the Knower and their ability to experience the transcendent nature of the Self.

It should not be considered normal for individuals to be over-whelmed by anxiety and depression nor for addiction and crime to be inevitable in our communities. Individuals should expect their

From Anxiety To Peace

creativity and wishes to be supported by society and their endeavours to support the lives of others. Full adult maturity includes so much more than is accepted today. We can grow beyond Paget's formal operations of cognitive development. TC is a normal experience and a necessary one to fully integrate the heart and mind. We need to look for new and higher rewards. We must look beyond material success. It is the nature of life to grow and the nature of consciousness to be creative. For life to be truly worth living we want success in our emotional and spiritual lives as well as the physical and economic. We need to find Carpenter's "deep, deep ocean of joy within".

An evolutionary leap to enlightenment

The level of self-referral consciousness, or consciousness in its simplest and purest state, represents a phase transition in our mental evolution. Sometimes evolution is incremental such as giraffes growing longer necks to reach higher foliage. But sometimes change is fast and gives rise to completely new possibilities. The human development of language was one such transition. The ability to experience pure consciousness is another. Looking further ahead the next one may be at the level of society and collective consciousness.

Peace of mind is one quality of an enlightened mind. Dynamism is also present. Activity is in tune with the surroundings, succeeding without friction or restraint. A sense of order within the self as well as between the self and the outside world is apparent. This precious concept is found throughout history from Lao Tzu to Emerson.

Regaining the role of the Knower

Self knowledge requires us to recapture the position of Knower. As patients and people who wish to remain healthy, we must strengthen this role in our Self and wrestle it away from the objective specialists. We need to have more useful, more direct, and deeper awareness of our own biological and mental intelligence. We must take awareness to the level of consciousness that underlies both physical and mental exist-

147

ence. From here the Knower has a reliable and complete view of all levels of life objective and subjective.

We have been familiar with waking, dreaming, and sleeping as different states of consciousness. As we become familiar with transcendental consciousness we find this underlying these three relative states. We become familiar with the very nature of consciousness, to be aware of itself. This self-referral property gives rise to the internal dynamics of awareness and the relationships between the Knower, process of Knowing, and Known. This abstract relationship is expressed in more concrete terms in the patterns of communication between doctors and patients.

In the traditional medical model the patient was merely the Known and was barely required to be awake at all. The many streams of psychiatry and psychology have worked to expand the consciousness of the patient and have him wake up to his potential. These include both putting the patient more in the Knower position and bringing the processes of knowledge and learning to the fore. The therapeutic relationship should serve to move a patient towards the position of wholeness. The patient should fully own all three aspects, the Knower, process of Knowing and the Known. Self knowledge has to become knowledge of the patient, by the patient and through their own consciousness.

We have seen that a major cause of mental distress is damage to the thinking process itself. If our thinking style is characterised by helplessness or catastrophic interpretation then we are creating a depressive or frightening world. We can use our intellect to watch and change such patterns. To do this we establish our perspective or Knower position at a level which is deeper or transcendental to our styles of thinking. The process of Knowing can then be observed and Known. This is a great benefit to having a human awareness. We can reflect on our own thinking processes and play around with all three aspects, Knower, Knowing and Known in our own mind. This game reaches its fulfilment as we transcend to pure consciousness which lies beyond the separation of Knower, Knowing and Known. This level of consciousness knows itself.

148

Being fully awake

There are many routes from anxiety to peace. Which one to take depends partly on where you are starting from or from what sort of anxiety you suffer. It also depends on what sort of vehicle you have, your personality and constitution.

The most important strategy for improving mental health is to experience the infinite field of peace at the basis of the mind. This place may be experienced in many ways through art, during exercise, or in relationships. The technique of TM is simply the easiest way to have this transcendent experience regularly and to mature quickly to a higher state of consciousness. This is the fulfilment of Behavior Therapy, to learn how to be at peace in any situation.

On the basis of expanded awareness we should use our intellect to dismiss unnecessary and unrealistic thoughts. Wherever thinking is negative or unsuccessful we should challenge this and not accept that being overshadowed by negativity is normal. When unity is more dominant in our minds the power of differences and conflicts to distress us becomes less.

We should always look to solve problems, treating difficulties as opportunities for growth. We remember that learning is natural to life and there is nothing we cannot accomplish through the expansion of awareness. As we achieve our goals we set higher standards.

In our relationships and others we do not have to accept that compromise is needed. We look to coherence allowing each individual's aspirations to be honoured while at the same time strengthening the cause of the group.

We respect our environment as the physiology of our collective consciousness. This includes the more obvious strategies regarding pollution and sustainability. We must also pay attention to the finer values of the environment such as beauty to sustain the more precious aspects of collective culture.

Along with direct experience of the Self we should keep in mind knowledge of our infinite potential and seek out more understanding of this remarkable truth. Others have made this journey and they can

149

be our inspiration. Some can also teach, with Maharishi being the prime example in recent times.

Illness can be extraordinarily complicated. Health is surprisingly simple. We can do simple things right. A balanced routine of sleeping, eating, and exercising is not difficult. Regular experience of the transcendent strengthens this natural rhythm. Knowing your constitution better through the language of Maharishi Ayur Veda allows you to make more use of your senses and your intellect to keep your physiology in balance with the environment.

To be in our usual waking state is not to be very awake. We can expand our waking awareness to integrate unconscious and pre-conscious knowledge. But to really switch on the lights we look to the field of consciousness itself. When we are aware of that field in which all our experience takes place, then we are truly awake. As Emerson said, nothing can bring you peace but yourself.

Modern psychiatry has become very optimistic. Even those who have suffered most severe anxieties should hope to have a life worth living. Do not accept that you are a nervous person. There are several roads from anxiety to peace. Our first goal is just relieving the mind from anxiety. The path continues until we have complete peace of mind at all times.

ΟΟΟΟΟΟ

Appendices

Appendix 1 Constitution Questionnaire:

Circle YES for all items that describe you as you have usually been throughout most of your adult life

	Vata	Pitta	Kapha
Walk very quickly	YES		
Thick, luxuriant, oily hair			YES
Dry rough skin	YES		
Reddish or freckled skin		YES	
Moist, oily skin			YES
Small teeth	YES		
Yellowish teeth		YES	
Large body frame			YES
Penetrating eyes		YES	
Quick, restless mind	YES		
Sharp intellect, aggressive		YES	
Calm, steady mind			YES
Thin, tend not to put on weight	YES		
Medium weight		YES	
Heavy, tend to put on weight easily			YES
Small body frame	YES		
Strong, large white teeth			YES
Dislike hot weather		YES	
Short-term memory better than long-term	YES		
Good overall memory		YES	
Sound sleep of average length		YES	
Sound heavy and long sleep			YES
Good appetite, cannot skip meals easily		YES	
Tend to be constipated, hard stools	YES		
Low strength and stamina	YES		
High stamina for exercise			YES
Physically very strong			YES
Easily excitable	YES		
Tend to get angry, lose temper under stress		YES	
Slow to get irritated			YES
Add the total for each column			
Doshas:	**Vata**	**Pitta**	**Kapha**

From Anxiety To Peace

Appendix 2 Influences on the three Doshas
Factors tending to increase or aggravate VATA
Dry, cold, windy weather
Early morning and late afternoon
Old age
Irregular routines, insufficient sleep
Suppression of natural urges
Weight loss
Falling
Excessive speaking, travel or exercise
Too little or irregular meals
Light, dry and cold food
Pungent, bitter, astringent tastes

Factors tending to increase or aggravate PITTA
Hot weather or excessive sun
Midday and midnight
Middle age
Late bed-time
Anger
Alcohol and **Tobacco**
Hot food and drink
Pungent sour and salty tastes

Factors tending to increase or aggravate KAPHA
Cold, wet weather
Morning and evening
Childhood
Excessive sleep
Too little exercise work or mental activity
Excessive food
Cold food and drink
Sweet, sour and salty tastes

Further Reading

General
Consciousness. Susan Blackmore. Oxford University Press 2005.

www.whatthebleep.com/ (Modern Physics)

Behavior Therapy
http://cognitivetherapyonline.com

The Anxiety and Worry Workbook: The Cognitive Behavioral Solution. David Clark and Aaron Beck. Guilford Press 2012.

Cognitive Therapy
Martin Seligman. Learned Optimism. Knopf 1991.

http://www.ccbt.co.uk/ (on-line mainly CBT, includes OCD)

Psychoanalysis and Dynamic Therapy
The Interpretation of Dreams. Sigmund Freud. Macmillan 1913.

Memories Dreams and Reflections. Carl Jung. Collins 1961.

Carl Rogers. On Becoming a Person. Constable 1961.

Biological Therapy
http://www.anxietyuk.org.uk/get-help/nice-guidelines/

Group Therapy
The Group Therapy Experience: From Theory To Practice. Dr. Louis R. Ormont

Natural Medicine

153

Healing Anxiety Naturally. Harold Bloomfield. Harper Perennial 1999.

Maharishi Ayurveda
A Woman's Best Medicine. Nancy Lonsdorf. Putnam 1993.

Perfect Health . Deepak Chopra. Harmony 2001.

www.alltm.org/ayurveda.html

Transcendental Meditation
Transcendence: Healing and Transformation Through Transcendental Meditation. Norman E Rosenthal . Penguin 2011

www.mum.edu/tm_research/research.html

Growing up Enlightened. Randi Nidich. MIU Press 1990

www.mum.edu/m_effect/index.html (Maharishi Effect)

Enlightenment
Science of Being and Art of Living: Transcendental Meditation. Maharishi Mahesh Yogi. Penguin 2001.

The Quantum Self. Danah Zohar. William Morrow 1990.

The Phenomenon of Man. Teilhard de Chardin. Harper and Row 1959.

www.sthapatyaveda.com/ (Sthapatya Veda)

www.ingramcontent.com/pod-product-compliance
Lightning Source LLC
Chambersburg PA
CBHW021146090426
42740CB00008B/968